Employee Theft Investigation

SECOND EDITION

Employee Theft Investigation
SECOND EDITION

J. Kirk Barefoot, C.P.P.

Butterworths
Boston London Singapore Sydney Toronto Wellington

Library of Congress Cataloging-in-Publication Data

Barefoot, J. Kirk.
    Employee theft investigation / J. Kirk Barefoot.—2nd ed.
        p.   cm.
    Includes bibliographical references.
    ISBN 0–409–90211–X
    1. Employee theft—Investigation.   I. Title.
HF5549.5.E43B37   1990
363.2'5962—dc20   89–25309
                                                       CIP

British Library Cataloguing in Publication Data
Barefoot, J. Kirk
    Employee theft investigation.—2nd. ed.
    1. Theft by personnel. Criminal investigation
    I. Title
    363.2'5

    ISBN 0–409–90211–X

Butterworth Publishers
80 Montvale Avenue
Stoneham, MA 02180

10 9 8 7 6 5 4 3 2 1

Printed in the United States of America

CONTENTS

ACKNOWLEDGMENTS

A special acknowledgment must be given for the many valuable suggestions made by Mr. George H. Harris, Director of Security, Ace Hardware Co. In addition to constructive criticism on the manuscript generally, Mr. Harris was of particular help with those sections pertaining to retail security activities.

Also, particular thanks go to Mr. John M. Haun, Jr., Manager of Corporate Accounting, Cluett, Peabody & Co., Inc. Mr. Haun gave valuable comments and help on the accounting portions of Chapter 1.

FOREWORD

Most would agree that in the past ten years, the world and how we perceive it has changed significantly. Accordingly, it is appropriate that *Employee Theft Investigation* be revised to address those changes relative to internal theft investigation.

One of the most productive tools for verifying admissions, determining value of goods stolen, locating stolen merchandise, and identifying co-offenders was the polygraph technique. Moreover, the polygraph as a pre-employment screening device was appropriately touted as being very effective in the first edition of *Employee Theft Investigation*. The Employee Polygraph Protection Act of 1988 (E.P.P.A.) nearly abolished applicant screening and severely restricted the use of polygraph in internal investigations. During this ten-year period (1979–1989), losses to U.S. businesses and bankruptcies traceable to internal theft have not diminished. The more astute companies continue to need alternative methods to address the pervasive problems associated with internal loss. Barefoot addresses these problems through his discussion of in-depth interviews, various controls, and paper-and-pencil honesty testing.

The greatest improvement Barefoot has made to *Employee Theft Investigation* is his insightful addition of a whole new chapter on investigation of workers' compensation cases. Very little has been written on this subject. Barefoot contends that in many companies the losses due to fraud and/or malingering in workers' compensation cases far exceed losses due to internal theft. In the majority of businesses, this is a neglected area that, at best, is handled administratively by the insurance department. The tangible and intangible costs can be significant enough to affect shareholders' value in a company and surely warrant investigation. There are few experts in this specialized type of investigation, but through his years of experience and documented results, the author of *Employee Theft Investigation* surely qualifies as an expert. In this revised version, he cites several actual cases as examples of workers' compensation investigations.

The bad news is that those who commit theft from their companies, be it time, merchandise, money, or through fraudulent claims, have become more cunning and sophisticated. The good news is that the author of *Employee Theft Investigation* has greatly improved his skills and knowledge, and in this revised edition of *Employee Theft Investigation,* he shares that knowledge and experience.

In the Foreword to the first edition, it was suggested that *Employee Theft Investigation* would appeal to three distinct audiences: professional security practitioners, the academic community, and senior business managers with profit-and-loss responsibilities. This revised edition remains a "must read" for those audiences.

Richard D. Paterson, CPP
Director, Corporate Security
McKesson Corporation
San Francisco, California

Introduction

INTERNAL THEFT: INTRODUCTION

Covington County, Alabama. On Thursday afternoon in mid-September several years ago, two men arrived by automobile at the Air Host Inn, adjacent to the Atlanta Airport in Atlanta, Georgia. After making proper inquiry at the desk, they proceeded to a guest room on the third floor where they met with a purported businessman who identified himself as "Doc" Long.

One of the two visitors was carrying a .44-caliber magnum Frontier Special tucked inside his waistband, concealed by a sport shirt. He was introduced to the occupant of the room by his companion and then proceeded to negotiate with "Doc" Long for the sale of ten thousand shirts. After haggling over prices that ranged from eighty-five cents to one dollar per shirt and discussing such trivia as whether the labels would remain intact or would be cut out, buyer and seller agreed on a price of one dollar per shirt (with labels).

An initial order of one thousand shirts and an "open to buy" on the remaining nine thousand was placed. Seven "samples" had been interjected into the meeting by the pistol-packing "salesman" as evidence of what the buyer might expect on receipt of his goods. The whole transaction consumed no more than thirty minutes.

At a price of one dollar per shirt, the conspirators were talking of a commodity that wholesaled at the time of the discussion for approximately four dollars and fifty cents and retailed for approximately nine dollars. This transaction was but the tip of an iceberg, part of a number of conspiracies and large-scale thefts that cost an Alabama shirt manufacturing company approximately one hundred thousand dollars in inventory losses for that year.

In addition to the gun-toting "salesman," the other two participants in the meeting were the company security agent working undercover along with another company security agent posing as the buyer of the shirts. There was no police, federal or otherwise, involved in the case at this point, nor need there have been. Yet, the case would ultimately result in approximately eight pleas or findings of guilty on federal conspiracy charges. Virtually all the participants drew penitentiary terms.

The "Theft Tax"

The above case is similar in many respects to thousands occurring all over the United States each year: the gigantic rip-off of American business and industry done to the detriment of the American public. There is an old adage that says nothing is inevitable except death and taxes. Whoever coined that phrase years ago undoubtedly had in mind taxes that are necessary to support the workings of government, education, and other public services. Without question, the pundit could not have foreseen a new tax that affects all of us today— namely the "theft tax."

Many authorities estimate that crime costs United States businesses approximately 40 billion dollars per year. One writer, R. A. Rupe, reported that the retail industry alone was estimating 8 billion dollars lost due to crime in 1980.[1] The results of this catastrophic disclosure take two forms: either business bankruptcy or an increase in consumer prices, which has been termed the "theft tax."

It must be recognized that all of the above figures are only estimated. Security authorities are quick to point out that these estimates are conservative in nature; if anything, the actual losses to United States businesses from internal crime could easily double the above figures. The truth of the matter is that there is no easy way to develop meaningful statistics for internal business crime. Most internal thefts are never reported to the police, and only a small percentage are ever reported to insurance carriers who normally provide fidelity bonds for the business community.

In an article in the June 1988 issue of *Security*, the magazine stated that "the U.S. Department of Justice now estimates that workers steal $50 billion each year from their employers."

In an earlier article, *U.S. News and World Report*, March 14, 1988, attributed statistics to the FBI claiming that fraud arrests in the U.S. had jumped 75 percent between 1976 and 1986. Embezzlement arrests in the same period rose only 26 percent.

The author recognizes that many of the fraud arrests cannot be classified under employee theft. But then again, the vast majority of frauds perpetrated within corporations and against those same corporations never result in an arrest! Perhaps the 75 percent increase is also true of employee frauds.

---

[1]R. A. Rupe, "Formula for Loss Prevention," *Retail Control* (March 1980), pp. 2–15.

Many larger companies, because of their size and their competitive positions in the marketplace, are able to absorb internal theft losses. At the beginning of each fiscal period, many companies, especially those in the retail trade, will budget a certain amount of money to cover operating losses due to theft of various forms. Such a reserve for theft becomes part of the company's regular operating budget, and the cost of their manufactured product or the selling price of their commodity is adjusted accordingly. Thus, in the end, the American consumer pays the so-called theft tax in the form of higher prices. These prices are passed along and added to by each segment of our consumer supply system: the manufacturer, the wholesaler, and the retailer.

The trend has not improved, nor has it even leveled off. Security experts have always agreed that there is a direct correlation between overall crime statistics and the amount of internal theft in the industry. In this context, it should be noted that the Uniform Crime Reports issued by the FBI show that larceny-theft in the period from January to December 1988, was up two percent over 1987. Although rising at a slower rate than reported in the first edition of this book, larceny continues to be a major problem for all consumers.

Corporate Theft Prevention

In the past decade or so, many companies have come to realize that there is more to be gained by taking action other than simply setting financial reserves and adjusting prices to cover the burden of internal crime. With the cost of labor, union settlements, and other aspects of the general inflationary spiral affecting the bottom line or profit figure more and more, companies have decided to attack the theft problem directly and thus put back into the profit picture some of the funds previously budgeted for write-off.

The past ten years have seen the creation of more and more internal or corporate-level security departments—departments designed not only to keep internal theft in bounds, but to reduce theft through preventive efforts coupled with a direct attack on the perpetrators themselves. Many of these corporate-level departments are now actually viewed as profit centers because of their success in preventing and rooting out entrenched thievery within a company.

Prevention efforts in setting up controls to thwart thievery are all well and good and become a necessary part of any well-balanced security program. However, corporate executives should recognize the fact that controls, preventive measures, and educational efforts are intended for the sixty or more percent of American workers who will occasionally yield to temptation if sufficient management controls are not exercised. At one end of this scale, we can find about twenty percent of the work force who need no controls and no restraints in order to maintain an acceptable degree of honesty. On the other end of the scale, there is an approximate twenty percent who generally pay little or no regard to preventive measures or educational efforts and who seem to operate on the philosophy that "whatever I can get away with is mine." People of this type will usually devote their mental energies to determining ways to circumvent controls that have been set up by management, or to taking advantage of certain weaknesses or loopholes they can spot. For these people, there is only one solution: detection, apprehension, and separation from the company's payroll. The subject of this text, internal loss investigation, is primarily concerned with this dishonest segment of the work force.

Factors in Internal Theft

Undoubtedly, a word of explanation is in order regarding some of the reasons for this nationwide problem of internal theft and the expertise that has been developed to counter it.

Population Shifts. Since World War II, great shifts in population within the United States have occurred. A number of factors have contributed to this movement, such as weather and the establishment in specific areas of key industries tied to national defense, the space program, or some other specialized national need. No longer is an employer able to determine the fitness of a job applicant based on his own knowledge of that person and the community from which he comes. More and more, the typical employer has been forced to make hiring decisions on the apparent ability of the person to perform the job, rather than being able to give any in-depth consideration to the individual's character and honesty traits.

Limitations of Reference Checking. Employers have generally become increasingly aware of the severe limitations of background investigation and, in particular, of the traditional reference letter, which means less and less as time goes on. Because of a fear of lawsuits, the overwhelming majority of today's employers are reluctant to give any information in a reference letter beyond dates of employment, job title, and salary level. More and more employers have turned to the use of such sophisticated screening devices as pre-employment polygraph testing or a paper-and-pencil honesty test such as the Reid Report[2] (see Chapter 12).

---

[2]Reid Psychological Systems, Chicago, Illinois. The Reid Report, developed in about 1947, is the original paper-and-pencil test designed to show "attitude towards honesty." It has undergone approximately 27 revisions.

Lack of Employee Loyalty. Unlike Japanese firms, which generally enjoy a high degree of loyalty on the part of their employees, the typical American employer has seen employee loyalty dwindle to the point where it can no longer be considered a viable factor in any well-balanced security program.

Much of this erosion of loyalty has been brought about by the labor unions that represent employees in their relationships with their employer. Many labor unions look upon workers as "their people" rather than employees of the particular company for which they work. Many labor locals have also interceded in company internal security matters to the extent that many employer investigations into internal theft problems have been completely disrupted or stopped in their tracks. Union business agents often inject themselves into these affairs by informing employees of "their rights." Many union constitutions or oaths of membership contain provisions prohibiting one union member from informing on another union member. All of these factors have contributed to the almost total lack of employee loyalty found in some companies and they complicate further the already complex approach to controlling internal theft.

Restrictions on Screening. Efforts of employers to screen job applicants are also hampered by various state-level privacy laws and restrictions imposed by the federal Equal Employment Opportunity Commission and local human rights commissions. After being investigated by either type of body, many employers will drop all pretense of screening job applicants and simply hire people at face value.

Lack of Security Expertise. It must be recognized that the typical American employer who has no professional security practitioner advice also has no particular expertise in the control and investigation of security matters and must depend more and more on professionals in the field.

Organized Crime. Other factors that enter into the complex problem of internal theft are organized crime and its various ramifications. There have been a number of reported instances where organized crime has attempted to infiltrate legitimate business. However, on an overall basis, the problem is not infiltration so much as it is organized crime's capacity to act as a fence for the sale of goods stolen from American business. In any scheme for grand theft of desirable products, ranging over a period of time, the chances are probably better than fifty percent that some segment of organized crime is involved in the sale of the stolen goods.

Drugs. The growing drug culture in our country today has also had an impact on American industry. We have seen a constant increase in trafficking in illegal drugs and other controlled substances within plants and stores. Many employees regularly conduct sales of all types of drugs to fellow employees on company premises. It is not at all uncommon to discover the use of marijuana and methamphetamine ("speed") on the job.

Gambling. Along with drugs, another theft-influencing factor that has been with American industry for a long time, and which has ties to organized crime, is the problem of in-plant gambling. Many plants and factories today are permeated with some form of the so-called numbers racket. Larger companies usually have one or more employees on the payroll who will regularly accept and place racing bets on any track in the country. In case after case, the author has found that wherever widespread gambling exists in a company, there is a direct correlation to the degree of internal theft.

Gambling, in this connection, does not include the annual World Series pool or other occasional office lotteries as having an adverse effect on employee honesty. We refer, rather, to the more sinister forms of gambling that can be linked directly to organized crime.

These, then, are some of the more complicating factors that the modern-day employer must face in attempting to control and ferret out theft within his organization.

Difference from Law Enforcement

When considering the foregoing factors influencing internal losses, one might immediately draw the conclusion that the work of the security professional is almost identical to that of law enforcement. It must be pointed out, however, that although the two are similar in nature and share many basics, there are great differences between the law enforcement approach to crime and the security specialist's approach to controlling internal loss.

The first and most prominent difference is that the police have as a number one objective the prosecution and, hopefully, removal of the offender from the streets, thus making the community a safer place in which to live. The number one objective of the security professional, on the other hand, is the separation of the offender from the company payroll, only occasionally resorting to prosecution. In doing this, the security professional makes a positive contribution to the bottom line of the P&L statement of the company. For this reason, and this reason alone, the police generally do not take an active interest in solving internal theft situations unless there is a concrete commitment from the employer to prosecute.

Additionally, it would be fair to state that most police departments do not have the manpower or the expertise to handle the intricate internal loss investigations demanded of the private security manager. The following case is a good example of manpower limitations.[3]

New York, New York. A high-priced specialty apparel store in New York City suddenly began experiencing obvious losses in men's clothing two and three times per week. A typical discovery was made by sales personnel arriving one morning when they noted that certain items of clothing were missing from the night before. The security department was notified. An investigation revealed a consistent pattern of mysterious disappearances in only the higher-priced men's suits, leather topcoats and jackets, etc. The losses appeared to be in a wide range of popular sizes.

The security department was convinced at the outset that the store was being burglarized at night and promptly made contact with the local police precinct. There was never any sign of forced entry, which made the problem even more perplexing and probably dampened the enthusiasm of the police.

The lieutenant in charge of the local precinct detectives advised that he would be happy to assign two men to assist in an all-night stakeout of the store, but because of manpower problems such assistance could be rendered for only one night. Unfortunately, nothing occurred on the night in question. Therefore, the security department was faced with the need to maintain the nightly stakeout within the store with its own personnel. The police did not completely lose interest in the case; they advised that, should the company security personnel succeed in apprehending anyone, they should call the police immediately and assistance would be rendered.

On the third night of the stakeout, the two burglars who had systematically looted the store suddenly appeared on the first floor, coming up through a tunnel broken into the bottom of one of the elevator shafts. The apprehensions were made and the offenders were prosecuted for burglary.

The assistance given by the police department amounted simply to transporting the prisoners to the precinct and handling the paperwork!

---

[3]This case occurred prior to the drastic manpower cuts of 1976 by the New York City Police Department, which were dictated by heavy budgetary cutbacks in all city departments.

SECTION 1

Indications of Theft

SECTION

CHAPTER 1

INVENTORY SHORTAGES

Security professionals generally agree that indications of theft almost always come about in one or more of the following three ways:

- Inventory shortages (or variances)
- Evidence or other symptoms discovered during facility inspections
- Information received.

These indications are the beginnings of a typical internal theft case, and we shall examine each of them in detail in the next three chapters.

INTRODUCTION TO INVENTORY

Many business executives hold to a time-honored belief that inventory shortages are valid barometers of just how a company is doing in relation to internal theft. Many seasoned security experts, however, are quick to point out that, while inventory shortages (occasionally referred to as variances) may be a primary and basic indicator of internal security problems, such shortages (along with overages) are subject to a wide range of variables. Any of these can influence the picture to such an extent that normal conclusions may often be completely invalid.

It is not the intention of this text to cover in anything but a superficial way the accounting complexities involved in inventory problems. For those approaching the subject with no training in accounting, however, some primary explanations of this very important aspect of loss prevention are essential.

Book and Physical Inventory

Basically, there are two kinds of inventory: the "book" inventory and the "physical" inventory. The book inventory is arrived at as follows: At the beginning of each fiscal year, a company will have arrived at a figure of its inventory on hand by adjusting its book inventory to agree with the value of the physical inventory counted at year-end. Throughout the year, certain purchases or production of additional inventory are made by the company. When received, these amounts are added to the beginning inventory figure. Also, sales of the company's products are made throughout the year, reducing the level of the company's inventory. Therefore, these sales must be subtracted from the other figures that are normally augmented by purchases or production.

At the closing of the fiscal year, the company has thus arrived at a certain figure that represents the beginning inventory, plus purchases and production, minus sales. This figure is known as the book inventory.

Once the book inventory is determined, virtually all companies are required to then make a physical count of all the inventory in their possession or under their control. This physical count may take several days and involve the efforts of many people. The figure resulting from the count gives the "physical" inventory. This physical inventory represents not what the company thinks it has on hand, but what it actually does have on hand. This count is compared to the book inventory.

Invariably, there will be unit differences between the physical inventory count and the book inventory figure. These differences can take the form of an overage or a shortage. Nominal differences or variances usually receive absolutely no attention, as they are considered normal for any business. Significant variances, however, whether they be overages or shortages, should be of concern to management.

Variances that are reflected as overages can be traced to a number of factors, such as price increases in commodities that went unrecorded in the books during the fiscal year, and also to inaccurate physical counts.

Shortages can also result from a variety of causes, including internal theft, undiscovered external thefts, human error, and, once again, incorrect physical counts. Other variances can be caused by incorrect compilation of the book inventory amount and improper cut-off procedures.

Possible Weaknesses in Physical Inventory

It would seem clear, then, that any security executive attempting to study and analyze the results of a particular inventory should always be concerned with the adequacy of the actual mechanics of the physical count. There are a number of good accounting texts, such as

Retail Accounting and Financial Control,[4] which cover the proper methods of taking a physical inventory.

The security executive should also be concerned with possible weaknesses in the system caused by deliberate actions on the part of one or more members of the physical inventory team. One question that should be asked is whether or not the primary counters of the inventory are the persons who could have been responsible for theft of that particular portion of the inventory they are now attempting to count. In numerous cases, key personnel have attempted to cover thefts throughout the year by padding inventory figures.

In most inventories, double counts are taken. It is essential that the security executive or accounting official make sure that there is no form of communication between the primary counting team and the second counting team. There have been occasions where the primary team, when finishing the count of a particular section of finished goods, would leave a number signifying the first count in a predetermined location in the section. This was done as a "favor" to the second team so that they would not have to make an actual physical count themselves.

As most inventory teams are constituted, each team makes initial counts in certain sections and then serves as a secondary counter for other sections. If all of the primary counters leave some kind of communication behind as to their count, then it becomes evident that no actual second count is ever taken. In this way, discrepancies between the first count and the second are never noted; thus a third and final count by members of management to verify a particular discrepancy is never made.

It is not difficult to visualize how an attitude of indifference on the part of certain workers could give rise to major inventory errors. One of the greatest deterrents to lax counting procedures by local personnel is a test count made by internal or external auditors. The mere presence of an auditor during the taking of a physical inventory certainly must have a beneficial effect. An auditor who takes nothing for granted and is aggressive and inquisitive by nature adds significantly to the integrity of the whole process.

INVENTORY IN MANUFACTURING

In manufacturing, there are two primary types of inventory with which the security executive must be concerned. These are raw materials and goods in the production line that are referred to as "in-

---

[4]Robert M. Kauffman, Gregory S. Finerty, James O. Eagan, and Robert M. Zimmerman, *Retail Accounting and Financial Control*, 5th ed. (New York: Wiley, 1990).

process." (Finished goods, which may be stored and warehoused at a factory location, will be covered under the heading "Distribution and Warehousing.")

Raw Materials

In the case of raw materials, the basic accounting steps are similar to those outlined earlier. At the beginning of the fiscal year, the company starts out with a certain amount of raw materials. Additional raw materials received by the company throughout the year are added to this amount. Those amounts of raw materials withdrawn for purposes of production are then subtracted from these figures.

If there is good record-keeping and a sense of responsibility on the part of workers and supervisors, the difference between book inventory and the physical inventory balances should not be large. At least it should be within acceptable tolerances, as there will always be a certain amount of waste in the production of goods from raw materials.

Accounting procedures have developed a standard for how much waste is tolerable, and therefore this is not too difficult to measure. "Standards" are used to record consumption, but any usage in excess of standard is recorded as a cost variance (not an inventory variance).

The following case, which involved two widely separated manufacturing locations, is an example of how an adverse human element may affect a manufacturer's inventory figures.

Saratoga, New York.   At a cloth mill that produced and processed cloth for overseas manufacturing, the night shift workers (and supervisors) seemed to be more intent on card-playing, drinking on the job, absenteeism, and general horseplay than they were on the task of faithfully producing the company's product.

Undercover investigation revealed that on numerous occasions, after a drinking bout, one or more of the workers would kick a defective totalizer on a certain cloth processing machine. The totalizer recorded the number of yards of cloth produced or run through that machine, and this figure was used to pay the workers for piece rates. It was also used in preparing shipping invoices to the overseas customer, to determine the total number of yards on a particular roll of cloth being shipped.

The workers discovered that kicking the defective totalizer would usually make it "jump" by 1,000 yards. In this way they would be able to show relatively good production for an eight-hour shift during which they might have worked only five or six hours.

On the receiving end of the operation was the overseas facility that received the yards of cloth. Not attending to details properly, the receivers would simply accept the yardage quoted by the cloth mill as being bona fide. A false figure was thus generated as to how much raw material had been received and was in inventory.

In-Process Goods

An in-process inventory is exactly what it implies: that amount of unfinished goods in the production pipeline at the time the plant is shut down for the annual physical inventory. This amount of goods is not normally excessive; it should be only, as indicated above, that amount in the manufacturing process on a particular day. Finished products coming off the end of the assembly line are often not recorded until a count is made for shipment into a central warehouse or distribution center.

Although in-process inventories have limited impact on financial statements and security considerations, they are also highly dependent on accurate production records and the integrity of the workers on the production line. Where component parts are being pilfered by production workers, many companies have instituted programs of lot control. Lot control, in its simplest form, means that at each major stage of the production system a particular lot must be fully accounted for before being passed on to the next major section of the production line. This means, theoretically, that there would be no missing components. In the garment industry, lot control has become a major importance in controlling in-process inventory shortages.

DISTRIBUTION AND WAREHOUSING

In distribution or warehousing, there are two major inventory considerations. First is the finished goods inventory, which results from the same basic accounting procedures discussed previously. Finished goods in a typical warehouse or distribution center should be influenced only by transactions that take place in the receiving and shipping departments. In other words, nothing should be added to the book inventory until it is actually physically received by the distribution center, and nothing should be subtracted from the book inventory until it is actually shipped out of the distribution center.

Concealed Shortages

The second area of concern to the security executive, and one not normally accounted for by standard inventory figures, is concealed shortages. A concealed shortage can be defined as a shortage of goods or inventory that is not obvious to the examining party.

Take as an example a liquor warehouse where cases of Scotch are being received. If a case has been tampered with and one bottle of Scotch removed, and the case shows no evidence of tampering, a concealed shortage exists. This may be discovered during the course of the fiscal year if the liquor warehouse has occasion to break open the case for the purpose of selling individual bottles to its customers. If this happens, the shortage is then noted and an appropriate adjustment can be made on the book inventory figures so as not to cause a physical shortage at the end of the year.

On the other hand, if the shortage is not discovered and the case is sold and shipped intact to a retail customer, the shortage is then discovered by the retailer. At this point the retailer asks for a credit adjustment on their account with the wholesaler. The credit adjustment is usually made, but the adjustment does not have any effect on the wholesaler's physical inventory. Unless a separate record is kept of all credit adjustments made throughout the year for concealed shortages, the security executive never obtains a true picture of what is transpiring in a particular distribution center.

In the apparel industry, the same type of situation can exist where items are normally packaged three or four to a box. When the order-picker is filling a customer's order and withdraws one item from a particular box, it is general practice to adjust the number on the outside of the box so that a subsequent order-picker will know that the box does not contain the full allotment of garments. If this is not done, through negligence, then the customer is shorted and credit adjustment must be made. In the case of pilferage from these boxes, the thieves usually do not bother to make notations of the quantity reductions in the box, and thus concealed shortages are created.

Of course, security executives will immediately recognize that the problem of concealed shortages may very well be on the other end—in the retailer's receiving room. For this reason, spot checks must frequently be made of boxes in a warehouse as well as occasional double-verified shipments to customers. Generally speaking, however, the accounting and security departments must be guided by what they feel are standards for their industry in the matter of concealed shortages. Oftentimes, deviations from the standard can be the tip-off that something is seriously wrong, as in the following case.

A moderate-sized shirt company was experiencing what appeared to be excessive concealed shortages in shipments of shirts to customers. As a standard, this particular company was compared to a larger shirt company within the same corporation that manufactured approximately three times the volume of the company in question. When these comparisons were made, it was found that the moderate-sized company had twice the amount of concealed shortages as its big brother, which was three times its size and in an identical business. With this kind of comparison, one can only conclude that there are major problems within the distribution or warehouse system itself.

RETAILING INVENTORIES

The very nature of the retail business dictates that inventory control and analysis are far more complex than for either manufacturing or distribution. In retailing, throughout the year there are annual sales, special sales, and many other factors which, if not recorded and handled properly, will have an adverse effect on inventory figures.

Shrinkage and Reserves

In retailing, inventory variances or shortages are referred to as "shrinkage." In virtually all retailing (and in some manufacturing companies as well) there is a psychological attitude that a certain amount of shrinkage is inevitable. As a result, the companies actually budget for a certain percentage of shrinkage throughout the year. In so doing, if their forecasts are correct, they do not close their books at the end of the year with a loss in inventory—a loss that would, of course, affect the bottom line of any profit-and-loss statement.

These shrinkage reserves vary from store to store and from one segment of the retail industry to another, depending on the type of business. For instance, in the conventional department store, reserves may be set up that provide for inventory losses of from one-and-a-half to three percent of the net sales. In the discount or mass merchandising segment of the retail industry, these reserves usually range from two to four percent. In clothing or specialty apparel stores, such reserves will usually range from one to two percent.

Shortage Reduction As Contribution to Profits

Some security directors have targeted their programs towards these reserves in an effort to bring the inventory results in under the figure that has been reserved. If the actual shortage is lower than the reserved shortage, the difference can rightly be claimed as a direct contribution to profits of the company. In other words, the company is bringing back into the profit column a certain portion of those reserves that were not utilized in covering for shortages that took place during the year. One major mail order house that also operates a large number of retail outlets has always taken great pride in announcing this actual favorable difference as a contribution to the profit picture of the company.

Theoretically, if buyers, merchandise managers, and other executives did the proper, error-free paperwork; if sales clerks did not make mistakes with customers; and if all internal and external thefts were completely obliterated, then there would be absolutely no so-called shrinkage. Accordingly, in the retail stores division of the author's former company, Cluett, Peabody & Co., Inc., it was publicly stated on many occasions that the goal of the specialty apparel stores in that division was a shrinkage of less than one percent. Several of the store groups within that division achieved that goal for two or three consecutive years.

Shortages Based on Daily Count

In some segments of the retail industry, stores sometimes make a daily count of major clothing items. These counts are normally made at the end of each selling day and should correspond to the amount of sales of a major clothing item such as women's dresses or men's suits for that particular day. Where problems are known to exist, an additional daily count is occasionally performed at the beginning of the selling day as well.

From time to time, these daily counts, although accurately reflecting the amount of shoplifting at a particular location, also may indicate problems within the store after closing. The following case history is an example of how a daily count inventory may add to the woes of the security manager.

Sherman Oaks, California.   Over a period of several months, the daily suit count of a clothing store showed significant discrepancies on an average of once or twice each week. In attempting to pinpoint the discrepancies, the security manager instituted an additional count at the beginning of each business day. The additional count continued to confirm the previous pattern and indicated that suits were disappearing from the store during the closing hours.

The security manager undertook a number of lines of investigation, including a secret audit of the alarm company records, surveillance of the store, installation of a hidden closed-circuit television camera designed to operate during the nighttime hours, and other measures. None of these efforts, over a period of weeks, revealed anything, nor did a minute examination of the actual alarm system and physical construction of the building by an expert brought in for that sole purpose.

Next came a further review and audit of the daily stock counts. It suddenly was apparent that discrepancies were occurring in the morning counts that were being taken by a relief manager who only worked in the store one or two days each week. The morning count would be at variance with the preceding evening count taken by the regular store manager or his assistant. On those days, the evening count would always balance with that day's morning count.

Interrogation, coupled with polygraph examination, revealed a pattern of dishonest salesmen and the assistant manager padding certain customer purchases. Padding was accomplished by adding extra garments to items being purchased legitimately. The resultant shortages were then covered up by the store manager in the daily counts he made, during which he "forced" the balances.

Although he was not personally involved in the thefts, the manager could not bring himself to admit, through his daily count, that there was anything wrong in his store. The discrepancies came to light only because the relief manager was making a completely honest count. In the meantime, thousands of dollars of men's suits had been lost through collusion. In addition, another considerable amount of money was expended for unproductive investigative efforts.

Point-of-Sales Inventory Control

In recent years, many of the larger retail operations have gone to a point-of-sale inventory control system. The system, in which all of the cash registers are tied to a programmed computer, not only records the sales that are made but subtracts the inventory on that particular stock item as it is sold. This makes for an accurate perpetual inventory control system and has the added features of a more direct security benefit.

Because the selling prices of stock items on sale have been previously entered into the computer, it is impossible to record a cash sale or a charge for that particular coded item unless the correct price is indicated. In other words, a lesser amount rung up on the cash register will fail to be accepted by the computer and the sale cannot be made. This eliminates, in large part, the old security hazard of under-ringing sales by a dishonest sales clerk. The only way this can be circumvented is if the sales clerk first punches in the code of a cheaper item of stock, which then is used as the basis of the cash transaction for the higher-priced item. This is the only way a dishonest sales clerk can pocket the overage but, here again, the dishonest clerk would have to have a list of cheaper items, and their codes, for that particular department.

INVENTORIES BASED ON ESTIMATED GROSS PROFIT

In many companies in the United States today, book inventories are not maintained in the manner described in this chapter. In the distribution field, because of the large amounts of goods that are warehoused and distributed, upward and downward price changes are not recorded on the books throughout the year unless, of course, the company controls its inventory figures by computer. Only in this way can a company with thousands and thousands of different items of merchandise be able to keep abreast of costs and price fluctuations.

One major distributor with nationwide operations, for example, stocked from twenty to twenty-five thousand different items of merchandise. It was virtually impossible to accurately record price fluctuations in book inventory throughout the year on every one of these products. Therefore, the company operated on what was termed an estimated gross profit. Estimated gross profits are simply arrived at by evaluating the actual gross profit percentages realized in prior years, and are based on what an intelligent appraisal of the company's business indicates will be the amount of gross profit.

"Cost of Sales" Category

In the manufacturing field, a similar estimate is sometimes referred to as a "standard" by which the company arrives at its gross margin of profit. In these situations, the basic accounting formulas described earlier are followed, except that a term known as "cost of sales" comes into play. Cost of sales in a manufacturing operation can be defined as all manufacturing costs incurred in finishing or producing a product. This includes raw materials, direct labor, and overhead costs. In wholesaling or distribution, cost of sales usually includes purchase price of the merchandise and any related transportation costs.

Where there are no proper records being kept, price fluctuations or shortages in goods from the manufacturing unit to the warehouse are simply absorbed into this accounting category known as cost of sales. When this system is utilized, the only standard by which a company can judge its performance is an estimated gross margin or gross profit, based on past performances.

Built-in Theft Factor

The security executive must be acutely aware of the fact that, where estimated gross margins are utilized, there is always the possibility of a built-in historical theft factor. As an example, when the author first joined McKesson and Robbins, Inc., the company's drug department was operating, and had always operated, on an estimated gross profit margin of about seventeen-and-a-half percent. After a security program was instituted and some long-term entrenched thieves were rooted out, gross profit margins started to rise suddenly to the area of eighteen to eighteen-and-a-half percent. This was astounding, considering the fact that for many years officials of the company had felt that a gross margin of seventeen-and-a-half percent was a normal standard for their business.

In other words, if there has been a level of theft that has remained fairly constant throughout the years, there would be no inventory shortages. It is only when people become greedy and begin to steal more than the historical amount that inventory shortages are discovered. The following case history is an example of an unusual situation where even an accelerated theft program did not show itself.

Seattle, Washington.   A theft ring of six men in a drug warehouse was suddenly discovered in January. The ring had been in operation for only six months and had been engaged in selling stolen pharmaceuticals to several drugstores in the metropolitan area. The ring had, by their own and two druggists' admissions, succeeded in smuggling out approximately $20,000 (in today's prices) in pharmaceuticals in the six-month period.

The company closed its books for the fiscal year on March 31 and at that time took a physical inventory. Because of the fact that the company was operating on an estimated gross profit, not only did the equivalent $20,000 in pharmaceuticals not show up as an inventory shortage, but the company actually showed a small overage on its books!

VARIANCES NOT CAUSED BY THEFT

As we have indicated indirectly throughout this chapter, there are many factors that can adversely affect inventory records, causing either overages or shortages. A comprehensive review of inventory problems must include some of the more common causes of variances that do not involve theft.

Price Changes

In the retail field, the changing of prices throughout the year is known as taking "mark-downs." These must be recorded in the books. Failure to record mark-downs properly in the book inventory will invariably cause shortages at the end of the year. Other price change considerations include mark-down cancellations, mark-ups, and mark-up cancellations. All of these procedures, if not properly recorded in the inventory books, will affect the book inventory at the end of the year in an up or down manner.

Receiving Short Shipments

Another vulnerable area in any business operation is the receiving room. Security executives are well aware of the practice of a dishonest truck driver attempting to divert the attention of a receiving clerk in order to retain one or more cases on the truck while the receiving clerk is led to believe that the count is accurate and that the correct number of cases in the shipment has been received. This practice is sometimes referred to as receiving "short shipments."

Also, there are frequent occasions when a receiving clerk will discover that a shipment is short but will not make note of it, failing to notify the accounting department accordingly. When this happens, the full shipment is put on the inventory books and an instant shortage is created.

A variation on this theme sometimes occurs whereby goods are received and then subsequently counted in a physical inventory but are not recorded on the books until after the physical inventory is taken. This, of course, creates a "cushion" and can help to cover up other wrongdoing that has taken place during the year. By the same token, however, it also creates an instant shortage in the subsequent year.

Breakage and Damage

Another area not to be overlooked is breakage and damaging of goods by rank-and-file employees. Many employees, wanting to avoid reprimands by their supervisor, will fail to report broken and damaged items and will simply discard the evidence into the trash. Where breakage and damage are not properly recorded so that proper book adjustments can be made, once again the inventory is shorted.

Unintentional Error

Last, but certainly not least, is human error. Indeed, it is probably one of the biggest factors of all. Unintentional under-ringing of sales to customers, the miscounting of goods in a customer's shipment, errors in typing, and endless other examples could be given of human error that can cause inventory shortages.[5]

ADVANTAGES OF DATA PROCESSING SYSTEMS

In many companies today, the security executive can use a data processing system to assist in determining trends in pilferage, etc. Many of these computer systems are used by companies for buying purposes only, and although they are not used for actual accounting records, in many cases they do constitute a perpetual inventory system. That is, on any given day, the computer may be able to indicate to a buyer or the security executive how much of a particular item of stock should be in the possession of the company and available for sale.

By simply monitoring the actual sales records of a particular item and then comparing them with the print-out of the data processing system or perpetual inventory, the security manager is often able to verify suspicions and confirm that theft is currently taking place. It goes without saying that data processing systems offer tremendous advantages in the control of internal theft without having to wait for the results of the annual year-end inventory.

---

[5]Additional specific examples are dramatized in an excellent film on the subject, entitled *Mission: Loss Prevention*, produced and distributed by the National Retail Merchants Association (NRMA), New York, New York.

CHAPTER 2

FACILITY INSPECTIONS AND LOSS PREVENTION SURVEYS

Most sophisticated security programs today include an on-going plan of security inspection of the company's various facilities. Admittedly, most of these inspections are devoted to a review of procedures in order to determine compliance with company policy. The aggressive security manager can, however, utilize these periodic security inspections to look for indications of theft within the operation.

It would be impossible in the confines of this text to outline specific indicators for every type of business. Each type of industry is different, and only by learning in detail the nature of a company's operation can the security manager hope to be able to arrive at certain indicators of theft. For the purpose of illustration, however, we shall attempt to point out common basic points of inspection plus some specific examples of vulnerable areas in certain specialized industries. From these examples it should be possible to develop some insight into how particular guidelines or indicators of theft can be compiled for a particular company.[6]

INSPECTIONS IN MANUFACTURING AND DISTRIBUTION

Records of Openings and Closings

Many facilities today are covered after-hours by an alarm system which may be monitored from a central station facility. Where central stations are utilized, it is almost always possible to arrange to receive reports from the alarm company of any unusual openings and closings outside of normal hours. These are often supplemental reports

---

[6]For a more in-depth discussion on how to prepare written security inspections or loss prevention surveys, the reader is referred to the text, *Corporate Security Administration and Management*, by J. Kirk Barefoot and David Maxwell (Stoneham, Mass.: Butterworths, 1987). Chapter 7, pp. 90–92.

prepared independently of the regular daily opening and closing reports provided by the alarm company.

In the case of installations with proprietary alarm systems, these systems may come equipped with an automatic printer or recorder that indicates not only the openings and closings of any doors in the installation, but also any tampering with the console or the printer.

For locations that cannot be covered by a central station system or a proprietary system with a built-in recorder, a time-recorder lock can be installed on the main entrance of the facility. The time-recorder lock in turn is tied to sequence locks on other doors. In this way, the security manager can obtain the same permanent record of unusual openings and closings offered by more sophisticated systems. This record can be invaluable when looking for a particular pattern of surreptitious entries or exits at the facility.

In addition to studying records of openings and closings for obvious holiday, Sunday, and nighttime openings, a security manager should also be alert to the extra two- or three-minute opening that occurs just after closing of the facility at the regularly scheduled time. Often, dishonest personnel have been known to place a cache of contraband near the exit and then re-enter the building within several minutes of its closing on the pretext of a forgotten hat, umbrella, handbag, or some other item. This pretext is usually employed for the benefit of a fellow worker who may have left the facility at the same time as the key-holder.

Where guards are on duty and change shifts at night, the situation becomes far more complicated. It is quite a common practice for some guards to arrive at their workplace anywhere from thirty to sixty minutes in advance of the relief time, and this may or may not precipitate an early departure by the guard being relieved. The problem, of course, comes about if there is collusion between the two guards and contraband is removed during the authorized opening of the door for the changing of the shifts. A solution for this is periodic surveillance of the facility at these times or the installation of a TV camera and VCR recorder set to operate during the opening period for the change of guards.

Employee Locker Inspections

Employee lockers are another very productive area that should be inspected in detail. Although it is unusual to find any hard evidence of theft in such locations, the security manager can frequently pick up other clear-cut indications of violations of company rules and regulations. Often, the major violators of certain rules can also be identified later among the dishonest employees of a location.

Alcohol. In particular, inspectors of lockers should be alert to alcoholic beverages, not necessarily stored in the original container. Many times, alcoholic beverages have been found in ordinary glass bottles, plastic containers, and thermos jugs.

Drugs. By the same token, many of the commonly used commercial drug preparations often can be found secreted in employee lockers. Here, though, the security representative must keep in mind that it is always possible the employee has a legitimate prescription for the drugs. This is especially true for the so-called uppers (amphetamines, etc.) or downers (barbiturates). On unidentified substances, the security manager should make an attempt to remove enough of the substance for laboratory analysis but at the same time should attempt to photograph the remainder. The time, date, place, and any witnesses to the search should also be noted. The most usual unidentified substance to be encountered will be the "nickel" or "dime" bags of marijuana, or possibly cocaine.

Gambling Items. Gambling records or paraphernalia may also be found in lockers. There may be memorandums of I.O.U.'s or rosters of players within a gambling pool where identification numbers are being utilized. On occasion, the paraphernalia for various athletic or payroll check pools may be found.

Evidence of Theft. As stated earlier, it is the exception rather than the rule that hard evidence of theft will be found in lockers. But sometimes packaging materials may be discovered that indicate that a finished product had been appropriated for personal use. The most common disposition of such materials is usually into a trash container. On occasion, certain wrappings or other identifying labels are discovered in employee lockers, especially if there is some indication that trash containers are being checked by management on a daily basis.

Legal Considerations. Under the existing body of United States labor law, the rule has been laid down clearly in case after case that, where an employer puts his employees on notice that lockers are subject to inspection and will be inspected, it becomes a management prerogative to do so. There is absolutely no question of invasion of privacy or unlawful search involved at this point.

The one consideration that may play a part in determining the method used for locker inspections is whether or not certain agreements have been made with the plant union on this subject. Some agreements provide that the employee must be present when his or her locker is inspected, and if not, then the fruits of any inspection cannot be held against the interests of the employee. In large plants, where it would be impractical for every employee to be present during a locker inspection, a compromise can often be worked out with the union to provide for a shop steward to act as an employee representative during an inspection.

At any rate, regardless of representation by or on behalf of the employees, locker inspections should be conducted without any prior warning and at irregular intervals. Private padlocks should be prohibited; lockers should be provided with locks that have duplicate keys for management or even a master key.

Many security managers, not wanting employees or unions to become alert to the discovery of theft, will conduct their own private locker inspections after working hours, in a surreptitious manner. The object here, of course, would not be to make a case against a particular employee, but only to give the security manager some intelligence as to what may or may not be happening in the plant. Decisions on official inspections, which by their very nature precipitate action against offending employees, should be made in a careful and considered way.

Work Stations

In most factories and distribution centers, employees have a particular area where they tend to accumulate personal effects over a period of time. Generally, this can be referred to as the employee's work station. At many work stations, there are desk drawers to be examined, the rear of file cabinet drawers, small boxes containing personal items, or other containers. Here again, the security manager should be alert to any evidence of gambling, packaging material, contraband, merchandise, or any form of illicit production records such as false shipping labels, false work orders, etc.

Sensitive Areas

Many plants and distribution centers have sensitive areas to which particular attention must be given during a security inspection. This includes special security rooms, security cages, and similar areas. Not only should desk drawers or file cabinets in areas of this type be closely examined, but also waste containers, as the following case history illustrates.

Cleveland, Ohio.   On a routine annual security inspection, a security manager inspected a security cage and noticed approximately six cardboard sleeves that normally were used to cover wristwatch boxes. Closer examination of the trash also revealed a number of empty watch boxes.

The discovery was made without alerting the order clerk. Therefore, it was possible to brief an undercover agent who had been assigned to the distribution center. The agent was able to gain access to the security cage, and he checked the trash container for several days, both at lunch time and at quitting time. It quickly became evident that an illicit traffic of from twelve to twenty-four stolen watches was in progress every day.

From here, it was a simple matter for the security manager to apprehend the order-filler who worked in the security cage as he departed the distribution center for lunch. At the time of his apprehension, he was wearing approximately twelve new watches on his arms. He was arrested and charged with grand larceny.

Lavatories

Inspections of lavatories, both men's and women's, are not to be overlooked, as they often prove productive in the revelation of indicators of theft. Particular attention should be given to toilet water tanks, not only the inside of the tank but also the space between the rear of the tank and the wall; the area underneath wash basins; and any small access doors to plumbing traps, etc. Shelving, ventilation duct work, dispensers of various types, as well as all types of refuse containers should be examined closely.

In a facility that stores or warehouses items of clothing such as hosiery, panty-hose, and underwear, the inspection should be particularly alert to old items of this type of clothing that may have been discarded in trash containers. It is quite common for women to discard worn panty-hose in trash containers in the women's lavatory and simply replace them with a new pair from stock. Usually, along with the old discarded pair, the security manager can also find the original packaging material in which the new product was contained.

Full Case Area

In distribution centers or warehouse areas, any security inspection should pay particular attention to the full case area. If full cases are utilized for picking purposes in filling customers' orders, normally such cases will have been removed from the full case area and can be found in an open stock or order-filling area. The security manager then can conduct a meaningful inspection of the remaining full case area.

Cases in the full case area should be intact and sealed. Dishonest employees will sometimes deliberately damage a full case with the forklift truck or some other object merely to make it easy to retrieve contraband from the container. The security manager should be particularly alert to any apparent damage to the cases to insure that the interior contents are still intact. In other areas of distribution, where customers' orders may be processed on the basis of three or four items to a smaller packing box, checks should be made of these containers to insure that no concealed shortage exists.

Miscellaneous Areas

Other areas that should not be overlooked by the security manager during periodic inspections are crawl spaces between buildings, air shafts, elevator pits, stairwells, roofs, utility or steam tunnels, etc.

In general, the security inspector should be watchful for any indications whatsoever within the facility of the existence of gambling, drinking on the job, or use of drugs. He or she should be alert to employees who appear to leave their workplaces for unauthorized reasons or proceed into unauthorized areas. Also, sleeping on the job as well as horseplay are often good barometers of the moral atmosphere within a plant. Many ingenious employees have devised methods of stacking full cases of merchandise to provide a hollow area within the stack in which they can drink, play cards, or just plain sleep during the day. The security manager who knows his installation knows the practices of such people and can usually succeed in discovering their secret hiding places.

INSPECTIONS IN RETAILING

The retail store has its own special peculiarities to consider during a security inspection. As in manufacturing and distribution locations, these retail peculiarities can give clear-cut indications of possible theft or rule violations that give rise to eventual theft. The specific type of retail establishment will determine the particular indications of problems with which the security manager must be concerned. There are common denominators, however, and it is useful to examine some of the more general aspects of what to look for in such an inspection.

As in manufacturing and distribution, areas of concern in retail security inspections include merchandise hidden in unlikely places, poor housekeeping, and of course a pattern of unusual opening and closing of the facilities, based on alarm company records.

Another area not to be overlooked, and one that applies to any type of business, is any indication of tampering with the alarm system. Detection of tampering requires actual testing of every opening in the building with the alarm company.

Surprise Cash Counts

Most retail security experts agree that the first item of business during a security inspection should be a surprise cash count on the various funds maintained in retail stores. Here, the security manager will be on the lookout for any shortages, in addition to post-dated checks, I.O.U.'s, and other unusual items found occasionally in cash drawers.

The security review should also include a study of the house accounts of the employees to determine any significant delinquencies. An attempt should also be made to ascertain whether certain employees have had wage garnishments or have made repeated requests for salary advances. All of these items can indicate that certain employees are in financial difficulties and should bear closer scrutiny on the part of the security manager.

"Hold" Merchandise

Virtually all retail companies have a stated policy on customer or employee "holds." Simply stated, this is merchandise desired for purchase by a particular customer or employee at a later date. It is set aside, usually in a rear stock room, and held for a stated period of time. Upon the expiration of this period, the merchandise should be promptly returned to stock for sale to someone else. In order to control this type of situation adequately, most retail companies have specified that "holds" are to be clearly identified with the customer or employee's name and the date on which the "hold" was taken from stock and placed in a non-selling area. The security manager then should carefully examine all of the "holds" bearing no names or dates or those with grossly expired dates.

Cash Register Irregularities

The retail security manager should be especially alert during security inspection to "no sales" showing on a cash register window—or, for that matter, any opening of cash drawers for no apparent purpose. This also includes the discovery of a cash drawer in an open position with no employee in immediate attendance. The security manager should also be alert to any blatant failure on the part of certain employees to follow house rules.

Proper Documentation

Two final areas that must be mentioned are a review of outgoing merchandise to determine whether any of it lacks proper documentation, and examination of merchandise in alteration departments to see that it has proper documentation.

Summary

In summary, the enterprising security manager in any type of business can utilize security inspections and loss prevention surveys not only to improve and maintain control procedures, but also to determine clear indicators of theft. In many cases, it may be possible to identify specific employees who are involved in some form of dishonest program.

After inventory shortages, then, the second method of detecting theft within an organization is the facility inspection. To these two indicators can be added a third: information received.

CHAPTER 3

INFORMATION RECEIVED

From Anonymous Letters and Telephone Calls

Most companies today periodically receive anonymous letters and telephone calls from outsiders. Some of these communications deal with complaints, some are veiled or open threats to the company. Others report crime or other internal wrongdoing. These reports are made by persons who may have good intentions but for reasons of their own choose not to become involved openly.

The task of the security director is to set up channels so that anonymous letters or telephone calls that deal with crime within the company are routed to his or her attention. In a large national corporation, the letter writer or caller often does not know to whom communications should be directed. Consequently, such communications are often directed to a local plant and may easily wind up being received by someone in middle management at that location. The security director must undertake an educational task to insure that information received in this fashion finds its way to the corporate security office.

At the outset, it must be recognized that anonymous letters and telephone calls dealing with security matters can have a variety of motivations. Knowing this, the security director must realize that some communications will be close to one hundred percent truthful, others may contain only partial truths, while others may be completely untruthful. A communication of the latter type can be motivated through personal hatred of one person for another. In some rare cases, certain false communications are designed simply to lead the security department on a wild-goose chase.

Each letter or telephone call must be analyzed carefully. The prudent security director of a national corporation will usually attempt to get some input into his or her evaluation attempt from a trustworthy key executive at the location in question. In spite of this, it is still possible to be misled by a communication if it is cleverly put together and takes advantage of local information and practices. The following case, involving both a letter and a phone call, will give a better idea of the type of communications that can be received, along with action taken.

Upstate New York.   In March, a handwritten letter addressed to the president of a major division of Cluett, Peabody and Co., Inc., was received at the division's executive offices in New York. (The handwritten letter is reproduced in printed form.) Exact names and locations have been omitted in order to save embarrassment to those persons implicated.

Cluett and Peabody

I'm might fed up to my ears with a bunch of rowdy jerks who come into my grill time after time trying to sell my customers shirts stolen from your Cluett's mill in _____. I refuse to be an accessory to their shady deals with stolen goods and I won't have my customers annoyed by these damn fools any longer. My wife and my kids say it's best to tell officials where the shirts are stolen from, maybe Cluett can put a scare to employees. It might stop and maybe my customers won't be pressured to buy stolen Cluett shirts any more. If I turn them in to the cops for sure these rowdies will burn my grill to the ground. Besides the cops bought some of their stolen shirts. They have the cops in their hands. M_____, who claims he is head security guard at Cluett, _____, and old man G_____ and P_____ are tough eggs. They have bad reputations around grills. When the old rowdies get together in my grill, all hell lets loose. They have some gall using my place to drum up customers to sell their stolen loot of shirts to. They interfere with my business and annoy my customers.

They've got some kind of shady deal going for themselves with some jane they call P_____ . She helps them sell shirts, according to P_____. He said this jane P_____ works with his wife in Cluett's and told me if it wasn't for his wife and this P_____ woman stealing a bunch of piece price tickets from a floorlady's desk safe, that old man G_____'s wife wouldn't have all the money G_____ says his wife has. G_____ likes to brag. P_____'s wife and this P_____'s woman must have stolen big loot, because G_____ says his wife is doomed to paying it back to P_____ for big favors. M_____ , your Security Guard, and these other two birds P_____ and G_____, sound like they have some big loot of stolen shirts. They claim that over the years their wives have stolen a shirt every day. They brag that they'll be living on the profit they expect to get off the sale of shirts they have stashed away on reserve for the rest of their lives. I don't want these rowdy, aggravating bitches selling their stolen loot in my grill. Customers back out the door when they see these bitches pressuring for a sale.

My wife and I are nervous wrecks. These Cluett crooks are hurting our business. We had it with you so-called Security Guard M_____ and G_____ and P_____. Like I said, if Cluett put a scare to their employees it might stop your crooks stealing shirts and maybe my regular customers can come to my grill for relaxation instead of Cluett's shirt sale pressure. The P_____ and G_____ women work in Cluett's laundry, _____. M_____ told my wife.

Discouraged Grill Owner

After conference with key local officials, it was decided that the letter seemed to be logical in nature and correct as to identification of persons and types of jobs which they held with the company. A quick preliminary investigation confirmed the possibility of the theft of piece rate tickets as stated in the third sentence of the second paragraph of the letter.

Ordinarily, this preliminary confirmation, along with other verifications received from key executives at the location, would have been sufficient to trigger investigation by the security department. In fact, preliminary plans for just such an investigation were taking shape when the location referred to in the letter received the following anonymous telephone call. The call was received by a middle-management executive approximately sixty days after receipt of the letter. The executive wrote a quick handwritten memo following the phone call and passed it to his superiors. It was then relayed to the corporate security office. The gist of the phone call, reproduced from the handwritten memo, was as follows:

Following is a summary of a telephone call received at approximately 11:20 A.M. on Thursday, May 22.

The caller, a woman, asked our switchboard operator for Mr. K_____. The operator directed the call to me, a common practice since Mr. K_____'s transfer to Pennsylvania. The caller said she wanted to "report a grand larceny," and went on to tell me about a man we have working for us in_____ who steals shirts on a regular basis and who has been doing so for some time, making a regular business of it. She said he wraps the shirts around his body and leaves by the garage door; the shirts are picked up by a man from New York City named Mr. G_____ (she could not spell it; this is the way it sounded to me), who pays our employee by check.

The caller went on to say that this employee should not be working when so many honest family men are out of work. She said this man has, over the years, molested many of our young female employees and has impregnated a few.

Although the woman was very well-spoken and had, in my opinion, thought out what she was saying, there was a certain emotion in her voice. I asked her if she had any personal reason for calling. She said "yes," that her daughter was pregnant by this man. I asked if she or her daughter planned any legal action against this man. She said "no." The caller identified the employee as R_____ S_____.

Early in the call I asked the woman for her name and again after she spoke of her daughter. She declined, saying that we could catch him if we watched him.

A._____

May 23

A massive investigation was begun shortly after the receipt of the telephone call. In the initial stages, investigators took the position that they were dealing with two separate cases at the same location.

Many months went by during an effort to corroborate the allegations raised in the initial anonymous letter, including an attempt to identify the bar and grill in question. Although there were twenty or thirty likely prospects in the area, it was never possible to identify a bar and grill that was operated by a husband-and-wife team and that was frequented by any of the suspects identified in the letter.

Concurrent with the investigators' attempts to identify the bar and grill, tail jobs were conducted on various persons mentioned in the letter and surveillances of several of the homes were carried out. Over these months, never once did any of these persons have occasion to get together or to meet. In fact, all of the people mentioned in the letter lived in widely separated parts of the community. They all had their own diverse social activities, and none of them ever came together in the evenings or after work. Some of the personalities involved were probably not even compatible, according to the results of the various surveillances.

On the other hand, the investigation of the suspect identified in the anonymous phone call was as productive as the investigation of the various suspects identified in the letter was unproductive. In fact, surveillance of the subject of the phone call led to the identification of other thieves in the plant. With the help of an undercover investigator, and extensive surveillance by additional investigators of the plant, automobiles, and suspects' homes, a very successful case was put together, one that identified approximately fifteen persons as being involved in heavy systematic thefts from the company.

The undercover investigation tended to clear the original subjects of the anonymous letter, with the exception of the guard M_____. In this case, it was not possible to corroborate the allegations, but undercover did establish conclusively that the guard was guilty of dereliction of duty. He regularly allowed his friends to exit without making the required package inspections. Other employees had their packages inspected as required.

No satisfactory explanation has ever been found for the letter. A number of theories have been put forth. One of them is that the letter was a deliberate and clever attempt to send the security department chasing after shadows.

From the Public

Strange as it may seem, there are still communities throughout the country today whose residents will occasionally come forward openly and are not afraid to "become involved." An example of the form such an open approach may take is presented in the following memorandum of a personal conversation with an ordinary citizen who gave information only out of a sense of what was the right thing to do.

> Mr. W_____ C_____:
>
> At your request, I am making this written record of a situation that occurred yesterday, Monday, June 7.
>
> About 8:30 A.M., Mrs. P_____ M_____ telephoned me and asked if I would stop by her office at the first convenient time while I was uptown at the Commercial Bank. Mrs. M_____ does the office work for W_____ Electric Co., this business is located next to the Commercial Bank parking lot. Upon leaving the Commercial Bank yesterday about 11:30 A.M., I went to see Mrs. M_____. She related this to me: A friend of hers, a man who lives in A_____, who does not work for (the company), told her that (company) distribution dept. (warehouse) employees put cases of shirts in his garage while he was away from home. When he returned home and found that cases of shirts had been placed in his garage, he immediately got in touch with a person or persons and the cases of shirts were removed from his garage.
>
> Mrs. M_____ said she did not know how (the company) could stay in business with stealing such as this going on.
>
> I did not press Mrs. M_____ for any names and expressed appreciation for the information.
>
> This information was given to Mr. E.B. B_____ and Mr. A.M. R orally yesterday.
>
> J.M.S.

Many security people will immediately wonder why the executive who conversed with the citizen did not attempt to obtain more details. However, the mere fact that the conversation was reduced to a memo and ultimately passed along to the corporate security department certainly made the whole effort worthwhile. The observation related by Mrs. M_____ was duly noted and catalogued for future reference.

Inasmuch as the information dovetailed with other data that had been received during the course of a major investigation, no immediate attempt was made to reinterview the woman. Through other means, the owners of the garage was identified. Ultimately he was interrogated and found to be involved on the periphery of a conspiracy to transport stolen property into interstate commerce. The garage owner, being involved to some extent, was used as a witness in federal court to assist in obtaining convictions.

The group involved had been transporting stolen shirts from Southern Alabama to both New Orleans and Grand Isle, Louisiana, where workers on an off-short oil rig participated in local distribution efforts. An analysis of the operation revealed that on only one occasion in a period of months did the gang members become so crowded for space in which to store stolen property that they found it necessary to utilize the garage in question. It was purely coincidence that the garage owner happened to be out of town at the time; had he been present, he would have given his permission readily for the use of the garage.

From Other Affected Departments

Experience has shown that the sales department within a company is the most likely to raise a warning signal regarding internal theft. In any high-volume theft operation, stolen items inevitably find their way into ordinary retail channels. These retail outlets are normally anything but prestigious stores—in fact, they tend to be on the low end of the retail spectrum. Nevertheless, once the stolen goods are placed in a retail location, that store becomes a competitor of the company's principal prestigious customers in that particular market area.

Stolen goods are usually underpriced in relation to legitimate merchandise, and it does not take long for normal customers to become aware of the fact that they not only have a new competitor for the line, but they are being undersold as well. Invariably, the first representative of the company to receive such a complaint will be the territory salesman. Prudent security executives will make the effort to establish a line of communication with their sales organization so that complaints of this type can filter back to the security department.

Occasionally, an investigation utilizing ordinary shopping techniques will discover that the low-priced merchandise was *not* stolen from within the company, nor was it hijacked. Rather, it is off-line merchandise that has found its way into a restricted market area, contrary to company policy.

By the same token, shopping investigations will often identify the merchandise as part of an interstate shipment reported stolen by a common carrier. This situation, of course, is not of primary concern to the security manager but rather is a case that can be passed along to the Federal Bureau of Investigation. In summary, all complaints of the above type received by territory salesmen should be looked into and an appropriate investigation conducted if warranted.

Sales departments are not the only segment of a company that may have occasion to stumble across outside information indicating internal thefts. This may even include the local plant security force, as evidenced in the following inter-office memorandum.

INTER-OFFICE MEMO

FROM: N_____ B_____   DATE: 6/8
TO: W_____ C_____
SUBJECT: Alleged unauthorized sale of shirts.
About two months ago H_____, our security guard, told me that his nephew, W_____, a farmer located a few miles south of _____, told him that he had been approached by H_____ W_____, son of the owner (T_____ W_____) of W_____'s Grocery and Service Station— allegedly a "joint" which is frequented by some of our male employees, principally out of the warehouse—beer drinking, gambling, etc.—who offered to sell him (W_____) some shirts which he had gotten from R_____ R_____, an employee of our warehouse. He claimed to have recently bought 40 shirts from R_____ for $40.00. W_____ didn't buy any.
Self-typed
No copies

E.B.B.

In analyzing the above memorandum, it is obvious that the executive who received the information simply sat on it and did nothing until his memory and sense of responsibility were apparently prodded by the receipt of other information, such as the phone call from a neighbor who had witnessed the garage storage incident.

From Employees

Many employees, believing that management does care about theft, will provide solid indicators if given an opportunity to communicate same. Here, whenever possible, the security manager should attempt to have these reports reduced to writing while details are still fresh in the minds of the witnesses. The following two handwritten reports (reproduced in printed form) are examples of the type of information that can be gathered through employees.

6-9

Dear Bill,
        Around the end of May, A_____ D_____, one of the clerks at the (company) Outlet Store, came to me to report that on two different occasions over the past several months two people had reported to him that they had been approached about buying dress shirts. The prices quoted were $1.50 each or 80¢ each if bought in lots of 100 or more. He was sworn to secrecy not to reveal the names of the persons reporting this to him. They both declared they would deny it if they

were asked about the situation. It was indicated they were afraid of physical harm if their names were involved.

Chris,

D_____ and I checked and double checked our shipment of shirts. We found another box (case) shipped to this store and as before this one was completely empty. It contained only the eight small shipping blue boxes. We (D_____ and I) counted our shirts individually twice and we both added them. We are exactly 121 shirts short. We came up with a total of 584 shirts out of 705. I included the 12 you carried back to A_____. Notice out of 48 short-sleeve shirts we have only 36. Will see you next week.

D_____ P_____
D_____ H_____

Received
June 7

All of the foregoing handwritten notes and memorandums-to-file could be replaced with a formal recording procedure utilizing an incident report form, such as shown in Figure 3.1.

In an effort to motivate rank-and-file employees to come forth not only with indicators of theft but with specific allegations, many corporations today have established reward programs for information received from employees. Normally, these reward offerings for internal theft are included in an overall program dealing with security. The subject of internal theft can be "cushioned" by including it with other security matters, as in the extract of a reward program from a major corporation shown in Figure 3.2.

⌐From Paid and Non-Paid Informants⌐

As any experienced security manager knows, dealing with informants is a risky, uncertain business at best. In evaluating tips received in this way, it is always necessary to ask what motivates an informant to give information. To analyze an informant's motives properly can mean the difference between spending a lot of unnecessary effort and being able to zero in on that portion of information that appears to be logical in nature. It has been the author's experience that information relayed by the average informant is, at best, only about fifty percent accurate.

Informants can act out of a wide variety of motives. Their motivations can range from hatred and vendettas against other employees or other persons, to jealousy, a desire to become ingratiated with key company officials, a simple desire for recognition, or even a hatred of law enforcement or security persons as evidenced by the occasional trap that is set up by an informant.

INCIDENT REPORT FORM

(For use in all company locations except retail stores)

WHAT:
Theft
- [ ] Employee
- [ ] Suspected Employee
- [ ] From Employee
- [ ] Checks
- [ ] Embezzlement
- [ ] Burglary/Robbery
- [ ] Attempted

Other
- [ ] _____

Shortages
- [ ] Transfer
- [ ] Receiving
- [ ] Delivery
- [ ] Money
- [ ] Myst. Disap.

Safety
- [ ] Accident
- [ ] Fire
- [ ] Glass

WHEN:
Date of report _____
Date of incident _____

WHERE:

Company _____
Location _____
City _____
Phone _____

WHO
Name
Address ____ Apt
City ____ State
Color | Height | Weight | Build | Hair | Eyes | Comp
Dob ____ Pob ____ Age ____ Sex
Emp
Address
City ____ State
Position ____ Length
SSN
Previous record

HOW (from the facts available describe fully HOW the incident happened or the method used. Time, place in bldg., etc.)

Dept | Description of Property | Value

REMARKS: (include any theory or supposition not revealed by facts. Also, names of witnesses or any other information which may prove helpful.)

Total

Distribution
- [ ] Local Mgr.
- [ ] Plant Sec. Official
- [ ] Regional Sec. Officer
- [ ] Corporate Sec. office
- [ ] Other _____
- [ ] Other _____

Disposition
Suspended _____
Ret. to duty _____
Discharged _____
Prosecuted _____
Other _____

Evidence at:
- [ ] Security Office
- [ ] P. Dept.
- [ ] Evidence # _____
- [ ] Returned to stock
- [ ] Other

Report prepared by _____
Title _____

CLP 3(8–73)

Figure 3.1   Incident report form.

Prudent practice dictates that, whenever an investigator is meeting and dealing with an unknown or new informant, a backup security person should be utilized. This is especially true for male agents meeting unknown female informants for the first time, or meeting any informants at night or in strange, out-of-the-way places.

Often, the security manager will be able to develop an informant within the company itself, especially when an occasion presents

The Retail Stores Division of
has established a
Loss Prevention Reward Program.

This provides you with an opportunity to help reduce our inventory shrinkage and share in substantial rewards. You can participate through awareness of the following:

Shoplifting:
Employees, other than management, assisting a person authorized to make store apprehensions are eligible for a reward when a shoplifter is apprehended and/or merchandise is recovered. (When more than one employee is involved, the reward will be pro-rated. See back of pamphlet for reward schedules.)

Charge Plates:
When you recover a company charge plate listed on the "Want List", you will receive $15.00. When circumstances warrant, (theft, fraud, etc.) an additional sum may be paid.

Errors:
When you provide information regarding a consistent pattern of errors resulting in loss of inventory and/or money, you will receive a reward.

Internal Theft:
While you are responsible for being alert to the security aspects of your specific job, there are many instances when extra awareness will result in the recovery of merchandise and/or money. When you supply such information, you are eligible for a reward.

Shoplifting and Charge Plate rewards will be paid you directly by your participating employer. In reporting Errors and/or Internal Theft, give the information directly to your company security officer, or if you wish, include all information in a letter, send via U.S. mail to:

Loss Prevention Reward Program
Retail Stores Division

If you wish to remain completely anonymous . . .

This is how the last page of your letter should appear after you have printed or typed the confidential information.

DO NOT SIGN YOUR NAME... but sign with any six digit number of your own choice. Tear off and keep an uneven corner of the last page, bearing the same number.

(choose your own number)
123456.

TEAR HERE ----

123456

Should you prefer to submit information by phone, call collect (312) 922-
Have all information at hand and your six digit number for identification.

After investigation, if the information you provided results in an apprehension and the recovery of merchandise and/or money, your six digit number will appear either in pay envelopes or a company publication.

When this occurs, mail your part of the letter to the same address for your award. If you wish to remain anonymous, use the return address of a friend, relative or other disinterested third party.

"Remember, any loss however slight, drastically affects profit, your pay and working conditions."

Figure 3.2   Example of a loss prevention reward program.

itself to apprehend some minor offender from among the employees. If handled properly, the offender can often be "turned" and then utilized over a period of time for valuable information.

The security manager must recognize, however, that the pressures involved in the "turning" are not long-lasting, as a rule, and must be supplanted by monetary considerations. In law enforcement, offenders are often "turned" with the implied threat of prosecution. This legal possibility has a lasting effect and most law enforcement persons can obtain a great deal of mileage from such a situation. The security manager, however, is not able to keep the specter of prosecution hanging over an offender's head. He must either prosecute on the offense in question or forget about it if it is allowed to languish. Thus, in order to maintain a reliable arrangement with the informant, a regular payment schedule of some type must be instituted.

It may surprise some to learn that many employee-informants will accept a personal check in payment for their information. These payments can best be handled by the security manager using his expense voucher reports rather than drawing cash funds from the company. A suggested procedure to be utilized on the expense report, in order to avoid identifying the informant, is to show only the amount, with an explanation, "Payment to informant for information received. Details in personal file." On the security manager's carbon copy of the expense report, which is retained by him, he can then list the name of the informant and whether a check or other written instrument was used. The canceled check may then be attached to the expense report copy as a supporting document. This procedure, if agreeable to the company, should also be acceptable to the Internal Revenue Service.

The following two handwritten reports (reproduced in printed form) serve as an example of how a minor employee offender can be "turned" into a paid informant. Instructions to the informant were that he was to report once or twice a week on any irregularities or wrongdoing within the facility. For these reports, he was paid a stated sum every week.

Wednesday Night
Oct. 27

Dear Sir,

Reason for no letters lately is because of nothing new to report to you. Things that I know of that has been happening lately is only small things. On Monday, Oct. 25 J＿＿＿ S＿＿＿ had on a short sleeve shirt and he was cold, so he found him a long sleeve shirt and put it on.

I didn't see J＿＿＿ L＿＿＿ take no shirts on Wed 27 but R＿＿ H＿＿＿ said he saw him take 10 of them. J＿＿＿ was telling me to day that he had to give a boy 10 shirts to get him to keep a 100 of them for him. Part of the 300 that him and B.K. was going to sell to your boy. Can tell you more about all of that when I see you. And that is about all I have for now.

Wed. 11-3

Dear Sir,

Today, Wed, 11-3 worked 2 hours over time, H_____ L_____ and I were sent to warehouse 7 to pull stock. H_____ said that he needed to get him some long sleeve shirts for him to ware this winter. So, I played along with him and told him that I needed some myself. So we got 9 shirts a piece and took them to his' house during the time we were working over time.

Also, A_____ J_____ got a small box full of shirts, and put them in his car. But didn't get a chance to get a count of them.

And also J_____ S_____ took him a shirt home with him.

Thats about all of this time

As events turned out, the informant was eventually requested to assist an organized gang of shirt thieves. He was to help steal an illicit order for ten thousand shirts which were to be shipped from Southern Alabama to Atlanta, Georgia. Ultimately, the informant's testimony was instrumental in obtaining convictions in federal court for conspiracy to transport stolen goods into interstate commerce. In cases of this type, the security manager must decide for himself what moral responsibility he has for the safety of his informant after bringing him into open court.

In summary, then, the security executive should be receptive to information from any and all sources. Sources that need cultivation should be cultivated. Other sources that require financial reward should be rewarded accordingly. Some information will be totally false and some information will be close to one hundred percent truthful, but the majority of information received will fall somewhere in between these two extremes. This middle area will test the logic and ingenuity of the recipient.

SECTION II

The Investigation

The Investigation

CHAPTER 4

INSIDE UNDERCOVER AGENTS

Having established that internal theft exists, only a naive management will attempt to solve the problem through deterrents and controls.

An enlightened executive group will correctly conclude that hard-core thievery is part of today's business environment. Accordingly, they will realize that identification of the offenders and their separation from the payroll are mandatory. Controls and deterrents are for those basically honest employees who remain.

Management should leave the methods and techniques of investigation to a professional. The security manager is ultimately held responsible for the successful conclusion of any case and should therefore be able to employ whatever legal investigative methods are indicated.

One of the oldest investigative approaches, second only to interrogation, is the use of undercover agents. Undercover investigation can be defined as a deep-as-possible penetration of the enemy (or opposition) and the gathering and evaluation of the information that then naturally flows. Many investigations today would be impossible without undercover, and any modern security operation should include it as a vital weapon in the war on internal theft.

SELECTING THE INDIVIDUAL FOR THE JOB

Among the several elements necessary for a successful undercover investigation is selection of the right type of individual for the correct job. Not only should the security manager give consideration to any particular skills necessary in the undercover role, but even more importantly, should be sure that the agent selected is able to blend in successfully with the work force.

For instance, in eastern Pennsylvania, sometimes referred to as "Pennsylvania Dutch Country," it would be futile to select any agent except someone of Pennsylvania Dutch background. By the same token, in a case where the majority of the workers are Chicanos or

Mexican-Americans, not only should the agent be able to speak Spanish but he or she should also be of that particular ethnic background. Work forces comprised of minority groups virtually dictate the use of an investigator from a similar minority group. Because of some of the ethnic background requirements of certain undercover operations, the security manager may find it necessary to attempt recruiting in certain limited geographical areas of the country in order to insure the hiring of a suitable agent. One advantage in dealing with a local agency, of course, is that such an agency can usually provide agents from the ethnic groups indigenous to the area.

Basic Qualifications

Regardless of ethnic or racial background, the good undercover agent usually possesses certain basic characteristics worthy of mention. The good agent should be a likable sort of person, possessing a pleasing personality, who basically likes people. He must possess a keen understanding of human nature, be perceptive and intelligent, and possess an above-average memory. The good agent will also have the ability to be successful at inductive reasoning.

Although it might seem from outward appearances that a good agent is anything but honest and loyal, these are two absolutely essential traits. Absolute honesty and loyalty to his employers, supervisors and to himself are necessary. These traits usually speak for themselves when, on the witness stand, the agent creates the impression of a completely credible witness.

Applicant Screening

Unfortunately, in view of the qualifications stressed above, a surprising percentage of undercover agents engaged in investigative work today in business and industry are *not* basically honest people. Experience has shown that where polygraph screening was utilized in the selection of agent applicants, a very high percentage of rejection was encountered. It is actually shocking to the uninformed to learn how many present-day agents have engaged in impermissible thievery, have retained and utilized drugs secured during an investigation, or who have periodically falsified reports and incriminated otherwise innocent employees.

Realistically, the selection of agents without these undesirable traits can be accomplished through the use of a written honesty test such as the Reid Report.

Inasmuch as most undercover operations are somewhat unrestrictive of the behavior of the agent while on assignment, it is necessary to place some safeguards for the protection of both management and employees as well as a control on the agent himself. This can best be accomplished by periodic interrogations. Where these are utilized, the following four questions should be included:

1. Did you keep an accurate account of all company merchandise you took on your last undercover assignment?
2. Did you pay for all company property you took and did not turn in on your last assignment?
3. Did you falsify any of your undercover reports on your last assignment?
4. Did you deliberately fail to report any significant security violations on your last assignment?

In-House vs. Agency Investigations

Along with the foregoing selection process, security managers of large corporations are occasionally tempted to try an in-house approach to undercover work. Many such executives have recruited graduating college seniors with degrees in criminal justice, industrial security, police science, or some related field. Experience has shown that there are pros and cons on both sides of the in-house vs. agency argument. Some of the differences security executives must be alert to are highlighted in the following comparison:

"OFF-THE-STREET" OPERATIVE	CRIMINAL JUSTICE GRADUATE
1. Usually good at "roping." (See section on "Roping.")	1. May be poor at "roping."
2. May not know legal aspects of the work.	2. Usually has insight into legal considerations.
3. May be a poor report writer, necessitating a rewriter.	3. Can usually write acceptable reports.
4. Sometimes makes a poor to fair impression on judge or jury.	4. Usually comes across as a professional in court.
5. Usually blends in and is "street wise."	5. May not blend in and is "straight."

The above comparisons are certainly not meant to be absolute, but rather are factors that occur at a rate greater than chance. Most deficiencies can be corrected through adequate training; even the lack of a formal college education can be offset by training and experience. Although a large company may be able to hire police science graduates, without question the only sensible route for the smaller company is to utilize agency operatives. Several large corporate security departments successfully utilize both.

Cover Stories

Cover stories are an extremely important part of any undercover operation. The more complex the case and the greater the sophistication of the criminal suspects, the more attention must be given to the preparation of the cover story. An agent can only be as effective as his cover story is acceptable. It must fit the role being played by the agent. Many authorities on undercover stress that there are three rules to observe on a cover story:

1.   Keep it simple.
2.   Keep it believable.
3.   Keep it as close to the truth as possible.

SUPERVISION AND COACHING

The amount of previous experience possessed by an undercover agent will determine the amount of coaching and direction he should be given by his supervisor. Many experienced agents are able to virtually take a case and work it singlehanded, with minimal or no supervision. The beginning agent, of course, will require the most supervision and direction, and the operative's handler must recognize this.

If the security manager is dealing through an agency rather than an in-house approach, he may conclude that he wants to participate in the direction and coaching of the agent who lacks experience. On the other hand, the security manager may have complete confidence in the agency and will be content to defer coaching and direction to agency supervision.

There is no set formula for the proper approach to coaching and direction. In some cases, several routine telephone conversations during the week, followed by a monthly meeting, may be sufficient. On the other hand, the security executive may well decide that the case is sufficiently complex to require meetings as frequently as once a week. A word of caution, however, is in order regarding the selection of a meeting site. Months and months of good, productive undercover investigation can be undone by the chance encounter of the agent and his supervisor with other employees of the plant in some restaurant, bar, or other public place. Although there is a tendency, on occasion, for the agent and supervisor to desire to get-together for dinner, it is best that any meetings be restricted to a motel room and preferably be held after dark.

"Roping"

The art of roping can be defined as the undercover agent's gaining the trust and confidence of a suspect to the point where the suspect will disclose past or current criminal acts, or at least will not hide them from the agent's view. Techniques used to accomplish roping need only steer clear of entrapment and areas of illegality. Roping suggests the old adage, "It takes a thief to catch a thief." The theory here is that an established, mature thief would never reveal himself to a newcomer (the undercover agent) until he feels that he (the agent) can be trusted or at least is not a threat. Therefore, if the agent can create the impression that he, too, is dishonest, he will have neutralized some of the defenses of the older thieves.

For all but the most experienced agent, roping is the one area that seems to require more push and direction on the part of the supervisor than any other. In this legally sensitive aspect of undercover operations, the agent must be prodded when necessary, but restrained when it would appear that his roping activities stray across the border into the area of entrapment.

Balance Between Two Employee Groups

Another area of coaching required by the inexperienced agent is the ability to avoid becoming identified too closely with any particular plant group. In any industrial setting one can usually identify two main groups of employees—those who are relatively "straight" and free from dishonesty, and those who care little about the company and take advantage of every opportunity to further their own ends either through company expense or outright illegality.

In the initial stages of an undercover investigation, it is often necessary for the agent to gain and keep the good will of the "straights." Members of this group often possess invaluable information about the illegal activities of persons in the other group. During this time the agent, in effect, must walk a tightrope between the two groups so as not to be identified too closely with either one to the detriment of his future relationship with the other. Eventually, the agent will have to decide to swing away from the "straight" group in order to become completely accepted by the thieves in the plant. This switching over from one group to the other is accomplished through the art of roping. It usually results in the alienation of the original group, which is loyal to the company and not interested in stealing.

Making "Buys"

Many agents must be coached not only in the art of making "buys" but also when to buy and what to buy. Newer agents often have a tendency to attempt "buys" simply for their own sake. No agent should ever attempt to buy contraband that he could easily obtain through his own efforts at theft. In other words, if the plant has a certain commodity that would be impossible for the agent to obtain through his own theft activities, then a "buy" would be logical. If the agent could obtain the item by stealing it himself, a "buy" would be completely illogical. It is sometimes easy to lose one's perspective when personally engaged in undercover work, and for this reason coaching on all of these points is highly desirable.

Outside Agents

The supervisor of the undercover case must also be the one to make the decision to introduce an outside agent. Many times, the inside undercover agent will be able to identify certain thieves among the work force but will not be in a position to further his investigation on the outside. Outside investigation can include "tail jobs" at quitting time and surveillances of subjects' homes. Obviously, these activities should never be attempted by the undercover agent because of the risk involved; they should be performed only by outside agents.

The director of the investigation is in the best position to determine when an outside agent should be added to the case. He must also determine the best method of communication between the undercover agent and the street agent for purposes of tailing. Usually, the inside undercover agent will be in a position to "finger" a particular suspect to the street agent as a suspect leaves the plant at either lunch time or quitting time.

Maintaining Perspective

The last (and most important) requirement for the undercover supervisor is that he maintain an overall perspective on the entire case. The typical undercover case will involve the identification of various

dishonest employees on the work force. This is usually done employee by employee. In other words, over a given period of time, the
undercover agent will gradually be able to identify more and more
of the dishonest employees on the company payroll. It is up to his
supervisor to insure that he does not become bogged down in his
relationship with any one dishonest employee or group of thieving
employees but endeavors to proceed and make new identifications,
even while maintaining contact with dishonest employees previously identified. By keeping the "big picture" in mind, the supervisor
sees to it that the case is developed to its logical conclusion so that
the majority of dishonest employees in the plant have been sufficiently identified to warrant interrogation.

COMMUNICATION WITH MANAGEMENT

It is virtually impossible to visualize any type of situation arising in
an undercover investigation wherein it would be necessary for the
agent to make direct contact with management regarding a progress
report on the case. In some limited situations, it may be permissible
for the agent to query management for additional information that
would be beneficial to him in his pursuit of the case.

Avoiding Premature Exposure

Occasionally, there is a tendency on the part of the inexperienced
agent to "push the panic button" and attempt to make direct contact
with management when he learns of some serious act of dishonesty
which is about to take place. Rather than notify management of such
an impending situation—which management is ill-equipped to handle anyway—the agent should be content to allow the situation to
proceed on its normal course and simply take full advantage of every
opportunity to gain information about the operation. To precipitate
an overt act on the part of management in attempting to thwart a
major theft, the agent would only insure the premature exposure of
the whole investigation and probably would preclude the eventual
identification of additional thieves.

Limited Progress Reports

Members of management should be made aware of internal undercover investigation on a "need-to-know" basis only. The reason for
this is not that management is to be mistrusted, but by furnishing

management with progress reports the security manager places them in the position of having to be expert actors, which they probably are not. No longer can management deal effectively and in a routine manner with employees who they now know have been identified as major perpetrators of theft. Even with coaching to the contrary, management has been placed in the position of having to put on an act in order to appear normal. This unnatural behavior can easily be detected by the rank-and-file employees.

Furthermore, there is a natural tendency on the part of management to attempt to correct or thwart bad situations or illegal acts. In attempting to stifle such an urge, once again the management person is put in the position of playing an unnatural role.

If progress reports are to be made, they should be in the form of verbal briefings to senior management only, rather than to operating management. These reports should be general in nature and should simply cover the general progress of the case to date.

One reason for excluding operating management from progress reports is that the security manager will not want any tightening of internal controls during the undercover phase of the case. Rather, it is desirable to have management slack off on their enforcement of their internal house rules so as to give the thieving group more opportunity for dishonest activities and to make it easier for the undercover investigator to do his job.

The ideal time for a more complete progress report would be on the eve of a major "bust," following the undercover phase of the investigation. In this way, management will feel that they are being included in the security efforts but will not be in a position to compromise or otherwise stifle the investigation, which has now been completed through the undercover efforts.

It cannot be stressed too forcefully that the most successful undercover cases have always operated on a "need-to-know" basis. The security agency supervisor obviously does not have as much ability to restrict this information as does the corporate security executive. The agency supervisor who presides over the client-agency relationship involving undercover agents can only counsel and attempt to educate the operating executives of his client about the adverse possibilities of premature actions on their part that could also result in serious consequences to the undercover agent himself.

Regardless of the approach, however, the fact remains that the majority of industrial theft cases today are being broken by undercover investigation. The security executive who avoids the use of undercover when it is clearly called for is simply failing to meet the greatest challenge head on.

CHAPTER 5

OUTSIDE UNDERCOVER
AGENTS

INFILTRATION

Outside undercover agents are normally utilized to complement the efforts of an inside agent or, in some cases where inside agents are not possible, to handle the investigation entirely from the "street." In the industrial setting, the "buy" may be the end product of the efforts of an outside undercover investigator, but basically his normal objective would be the infiltration of designated places and/or certain groups of people.

Cover Stories

Unlike the elaborate precautions and efforts directed at setting up a cover for the inside undercover agent, the external or outside undercover agent can often get by with a cover story that will withstand only a cursory inspection.

An individual cover story for an outside undercover agent, like that for an inside agent, has to be designed to take into account any complexities of the case and, of course, must be in keeping with the projected time span of the investigation. In other words, the more serious the case, the more effort will generally be put into establishing an individual cover. The most difficult cover stories will be those that must be constructed for "street" agents who plan to work in small rural communities where everyone is either known to or at least generally recognized by most of the local residents. The following extract of a case history offers an example of how such a group cover story can be put together.

Bartow County, Georgia. After an initial inside undercover investigation had proved successful, it was decided to supplement the inside agent's efforts with a team of outside undercover investigators. The purpose of the outside team was primarily that of surveillance of various M.O.'s, or methods of operation, which the inside agent had discovered were being utilized to remove stolen merchandise.

The team, consisting of two males and one female, headquartered at a local motel which catered to construction crews for the power company and the railroad. The cover was simple and to the point—the team claimed to be from a survey company engaged in environmental studies. Specifically, they were supposedly making an air pollution study of the area in relation to the numerous fabric and textile mills which are located in the county. This story was augmented by appropriate signs on the surveillance van, company name tags, and safety hats with company insignia. The surveillance was programmed to run for a period of six weeks and was successful in a community that normally would be somewhat suspicious of out-of-town strangers.

Another successful group cover story has been an engineering survey team, complete with some of the equipment "props" normally associated with engineering field survey work. As in all undercover work, the possibilities of adequate cover stories to fit the particular situation are only limited by one's imagination.

Infiltration Leading Up to the "Buy"

As an example of how certain places and groups of people may be infiltrated, the following case history reveals the events and efforts leading up to the "buy" that was described in the Introduction.

Covington County, Alabama.   Through the efforts of one outside agent who was working undercover as a local taxicab driver, investigators were able to pinpoint a local private club as a hang-out for most of the criminal element in the community. It was felt that, by infiltrating such a place, an agent could pick up a trail in connection with stolen shirts. A second agent was therefore assigned the task of penetrating the club.

On his first several visits he was able to gain admission but was unable to strike up any conversations of note and generally was received coolly. On both of his early visits to the club, the agent noticed a young lady patron whom he had previously observed working in the community. He made it a point to meet this young lady outside of the environs of the club and make her acquaintance. After a short time, the two began dating. At the young lady's suggestion, they began spending a number of their evenings at the club, which was her favorite spot for social activities.

The agent had previously observed that the young lady was very friendly with the bartender, the bouncer, and other regulars of the establishment. Through her, he became friendly with the club's bouncer and was eventually accepted as a "regular" himself. The bouncer ultimately became the pistol-packing "salesman" who took part in the conspiracy to sell ten thousand shirts at a meeting at the Atlanta Airport. He was not an employee of the company, but through his fencing activities on behalf of the employee theft ring, the direct link was made.

Transportation

In any infiltration of a small rural community, transportation can be a problem. Experience has shown that the use of late model rental cars is completely counterproductive, as these generally tend to be associated in local residents' minds with the type of transportation used by federal agents.

If a moving surveillance is to be conducted, then the investigator should utilize slightly older model automobiles that are in excellent mechanical condition. If moving surveillance is not a critical point in the case and the vehicle is needed to provide transportation only, then even older cars can be procured, as long as they are basically in keeping with the cover story which has been set up. Registration of the vehicles can either be in the names of the individual agents or in the name of the "cover" company, e.g., "Atwell Survey Co." Insurance coverage can usually be accomplished by the corporate insurance department's simply adding such cars to the listing furnished to the insurance carrier. If the corporation is self-insured, then independent liability insurance should be purchased.

With the advent of the CB radio boom in the United States, the appearance of a whip antenna with magnetic base on the roof top of an older model car raises little or no suspicion. Furthermore, it enables the investigators to conduct their surveillance using their own security radios, which will normally be in the UHF ranges.

MAKING THE "BUY"

A "buy" in the corporate security field may encompass two purposes:

1. To obtain the physical evidence of the crime.
2. To enable the investigators to determine the actual method utilized in removing the goods.

Many times, because of his isolated work assignment, an inside undercover investigator is unable to discover the actual M.O. used by the thieves. In order to gain this information, he has to depend on an order for a "buy" to generate enough activity so that the street agent can observe the method utilized.

Many times, the "buy" can be initiated by the inside undercover agent himself. That is, the inside agent can offer to introduce company thieves, whom he has already identified, to an "acquaintance" who is in the market for stolen goods. This offer cannot be construed as entrapment if the agent has already been able to establish a pattern of theft. The courts have generally held that such an offer is merely giving the thieves an additional opportunity to carry forth a scheme that had already been in existence. As pointed out earlier, the inside agent should never attempt to make a "buy" of something that he himself could steal as easily as the thieves.

Photographing and Recording

If the agent is successful in interesting the thieves in discussing a "buy" with his "acquaintance," every effort should be made, consistent with legality, to obtain evidence of such a meeting. Motion pictures or still photos may be taken of the participants of the meeting as they arrive at a designated place. Actual "bugging" of the room in question or even of one of the undercover participants is also desirable. Unless a particular state law forbids all electronic surveillance, bugging a room or "wiring up" an agent does not violate the law, as long as it is the agent's room and/or the agent is a party to the conversation with the subject. Tape recordings of such a meeting are often valuable in court if the meeting is handled properly and the recording itself is of good quality.

Such meetings should usually be held on apparently "neutral" ground, and in places that would minimize the chances for injury to the participants and maximize the opportunities for photographic or recording coverage. Motel rooms usually prove ideal for this type of activity. Figures 5.1 and 5.2 are examples of photographic corroboration of a "buy."

Negotiating With the Thieves

The second agent, posing as the fence, should be an excellent actor and be able to negotiate with the thieves much as any merchant would who was engaged in buying stolen merchandise. If the agent seems too eager to buy, the whole deal can be jeopardized. For this reason, he should appear to be reluctant to part with his money unless there is absolutely no question of getting adequate value in return.

Figure 5.1 Photograph taken by an investigator just after a "buy" has been made. Goods have already been transferred to trunk of courier's car.

Agents entering into such negotiations should be well versed in the true value of the items for which they are negotiating. Generally speaking, no more than 25 percent of the indicated retail price should ever be paid for stolen goods. Actually, the price paid can be an even lower percentage, depending on the quantity of goods to be ordered and also whether there are any unusual circumstances that would put the thieves in a position of wanting to make a very fast sale. The agent making the "buy" should not hesitate to haggle over minor details as any dishonest merchant would be likely to do. For instance, a discussion about whether or not labels have to be destroyed can often contribute to the overall roping effort, and in some cases may also contribute to a reduction in price if the labels are to be removed by the buyer.

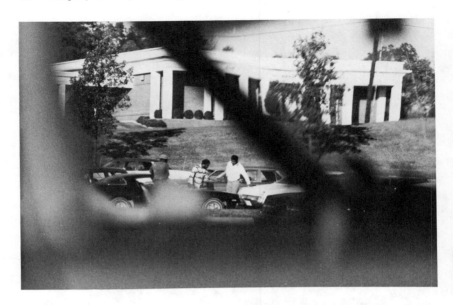

Figure 5.2 Photograph taken through windshield of surveillance vehicle shows participants in a "buy" haggling over price.

Before the meeting takes place, the buying agent should also insist that the thieves produce samples of the product they intend to sell at the meeting. If such samples are not forthcoming, the buyer should insist upon delivery of the samples prior to any deal being consummated and the money changing hands.

Eliminating the "Middle Man"

One favorite tactic of many security chiefs is to have the second agent, posing as the buyer, attempt to eliminate the inside undercover agent from any further transactions. Generally, this is easily accomplished by the second agent's simply saying to the thieves, "Why don't we deal direct—we would all make more money by letting John out of it." Most thieves will jump at the chance to eliminate a "middle man" and save any "cut" they feel they might have to pass along. They usually explain this away by later telling the inside agent that negotiations have fallen through and that no deal is possible. They assume, of course, that the buyer will hold up his end of the story should the inside agent check back for its truthfulness.

By severing the inside agent from further transactions, the risk of losing the case through charges of entrapment is greatly reduced.

The whole idea is to attempt to be able to show that the actual stealing of the goods by the thieves is not being influenced by the inside undercover agent, and that the "buy" itself represents nothing more than an additional outlet for the thieves to make their sale.

Precautions Against Robbery

As in law enforcement cases, great caution must be used when the actual "buy" itself takes place. The thieves know that the buyer or his "courier" or pick-up man will usually be carrying a large amount of cash. It is not uncommon to encounter thieves with such short-sightedness that they attempt to rob the pick-up man of the money and deliver absolutely no goods whatsoever. This can sometimes be circumvented by having the "buy" itself covered by ample under-cover agents in the vicinity, whose very presence tends to discourage an armed robbery but would not be counterproductive insofar as the actual "buy" is concerned. On some occasions, where an inside undercover agent has been close to the theft group, it is possible to learn of holdup plans beforehand and to take adequate precaution.

In the event that a holdup does take place, the pick-up man should be instructed to cooperate to the fullest and simply hand over the money. With ample witnesses in the locale, it would then be an easy matter to file armed robbery charges against the thieves at the appropriate time. Armed robbery usually carries a much greater pen-alty than grand larceny and is just as effective a method of separating wrongdoers from a company payroll as any other.

In arranging for the "buy" to take place, common sense will dictate the selection of a location that is in the open, has at least some people in the area, and is in daylight. All of these things may not always be possible but certainly are highly desirable from the standpoint of the security manager.

Another precautionary tactic employed from time to time with success is that of "buying short." In the industrial setting, the security manager is utilizing company funds to pay for company merchandise that has already been stolen; naturally, he will want to minimize the expenditure of such funds. The way to do this is for the buying agent to simply give his pick-up man less cash than was agreed upon, with instructions to bring back fewer goods. After all, the ultimate objec-tive here is simply to secure some of the goods as evidence, and it is reasonable to assume that many of the remaining goods can be recovered through a search warrant or consent to search.

"Buying short" involves a certain risk of alienating the thieves to the point where the transaction may not be completed. An astute security manager, however, knowing the psychological make-up of the thieves with whom he is dealing, can usually be successful in projecting the outcome; namely, that the thieves will take the position that some money is better than no money and that they have been able to move at least some of their stolen goods. If the "buying short" tactic is used, however, the thieves should be left with the clear impression that more "buys" are to come and ultimately they will be able to sell the original quantity of goods that was discussed.

Transporting Contraband

In planning for the transportation of contraband from a "buy," security personnel should be careful not to utilize personal automobiles if there is a chance that the vehicles would be traceable and would compromise the investigation in some way or endanger the operative. Generally speaking, a rental car or truck that cannot be traced is the most desirable way of picking up contraband and transporting it from the scene to the location where it will be held.

Preservation of Evidence

The rules involving the preservation of evidence obtained through "buys" or any other means are no different for industrial security personnel than for law enforcement personnel. The chain of possession of such evidence must be clearly shown to the satisfaction of any judge or arbitrator. This is simply accomplished by having the pick-up man (using the foregoing discussion as an example) place his initials and the date and time on the cartons or containers as quickly as it is convenient for him to do so without jeopardizing his cover. If the pick-up man then turns the goods over to another security person who has been designated to maintain custody of the contraband, then that agent must also indicate on the container his initials, the time, and the date he takes a receipt from the first agent.

The main point is to be able to show who had sole custody of the goods during any given time span, and to prove that no one else was in a position to tamper with or alter the evidence in any way. It is also suggested that the written report of the agent involved in the handling of the contraband should indicate the marking of such evidence for identification. If possible, the nature of the identifying marks and their location on the contraband should be included. In this way the written report stands to corroborate the actual identification mark on the evidence and thus greatly bolsters the entire case.

"Switching" Contraband

A very valuable approach to obtaining physical evidence of theft can sometimes be worked out between an inside undercover agent and a "street" agent who, working as a team, can endeavor to "switch" stolen merchandise. An example of this is a situation where the inside undercover agent has positively identified a fellow employee as regularly stealing certain items of company property. If the thief in question frequents a tavern or some other location such as a pool hall after work, he may be in the habit of carrying the stolen items with him in a paper bag or some other container. It is sometimes possible to switch paper bags or other similar containers, leaving ones filled with fruit or some other innocuous items in place of those filled with contraband. The stolen merchandise thus seized can later be used as a basis for a specific complaint of larceny on that date. Experience has shown that when such switches are made, the thief usually concludes that the mix-up was the result of a natural mistake.

Seizure of Company Property

On some occasions, it may be possible to "steal back" or seize company property that is in the process of being removed. An example of this is where certain stolen items are placed in the bed of a pickup truck parked in the company parking lot. If the opportunity presents itself, an outside "street" agent can sometimes remove one or two of the specific stolen items from the bed of the truck. At the worst, the thief will conclude that part of his load has been "ripped off" by another thieving employee. From the agent's standpoint, he now has gained possession of some actual physical evidence of larceny that can be charged to the suspect.

Marking Contraband

On other occasions where it is not possible to make switches or seizures, either the inside or the outside agent may be in a position to mark the contraband for future identification should it be recovered during a subsequent search. This is most easily accomplished by utilizing a fluorescent crayon, which can be obtained from any police supply company. If the crayon is not available, then any identifying mark, even with a ballpoint pen, can be made by the undercover agent.

    In one case where systematic stealing was in progress over a period of months and the only desire was to mark the evidence, a special rubber stamp was made up signifying "Nov. 31." This was used to stamp cartons and aroused absolutely no suspicion on the part of the thieves involved in the operation. Of course, such a date does not exist, and therefore the unique stamp became an identification mark that would easily hold up in court.

SHOPPING INVESTIGATIONS

A major form of street type undercover investigations utilized today is called "shopping." Shopping investigators are used primarily to service the retail store industry but may also be utilized in other types of establishments such as restaurants, hotels, bars, etc. For purposes of illustration, however, we shall restrict our discussion to shopping investigations directed toward the retail store industry.

Shopping investigations are offered by a number of private agencies around the country who service the retail field. In recent years, a number of larger retail companies have undertaken shopping investigations on an in-house basis.

Service and Integrity Shopping

Basically, shopping investigations can be broken down into two types: service shopping and integrity shopping. The old rationale behind service and integrity shopping was that they provided management with a tool to evaluate the type of service being rendered by the salespeople to the customer (service shopping) as well as an honesty test of the personnel themselves (integrity shopping). Many security chiefs in recent years have come to question the advisability of combining the two types of shopping into one investigation. In increasing numbers, retail security managers have come to the conclusion that integrity shopping is compromised or weakened to some extent when it is combined with service shopping. The reason for this is that the investigator must give so much concentration to the reporting aspects of the service shopping that he is unable to devote sufficient attention to the techniques needed to insure a good integrity "shop." Furthermore, many members of shopping investigation teams are excellent at service shopping but are poor producers when it comes to making integrity "shops."

Integrity Shopping Techniques

Essentially, an integrity "shop" can be defined as creating an atmosphere in which the sales clerk will be likely to commit a dis-

SAMPLE SHOPPING INVESTIGATION REPORT

FIRM_____ Store No._____ Case No._____

Address_____ City_____ State_____

Date_____ Time_____ am pm Opr._____ Report No._____

NAME
NUMBER
LETTER_____

Reg loc/no:_____

Sex_____ Age_____

Reg read:_____

Height_____ Weight_____

Other cust/oprs/salespeople:_____

Build_____

PAYMENT MADE								
$20	$10	$5	$1	50¢	25¢	10¢	5¢	1¢

1.Pur   Trans #___

Eyes_____ Nose_____   2.Pur   Trans #___

Teeth_____

DESCRIPTION OF TRANSACTION

Complexion_____

Hair color_____

How combed_____

Glasses_____

Jewelry_____

Other_____

SALESPERSONS APPEARANCE:

____ Well groomed
____ Passible
____ Average
____ Unimpressive
____ Unkempt
____ Other

SALESPERSONS ATTITUDE:

____ Enthusiastic
____ Pleasant
____ Routine
____ Indifferent
____ Antagonistic
____ Served promptly
____ Suggested other items
____ Offered a 'thank you'
____ Other

PURCHASES MADE

TOTAL

Figure 5.3   Sample shopping investigation report.

honest act if he or she has the propensity to do so. Here again, this is not to be confused with entrapment. Integrity shopping gives the thieving employee an opportunity to do the very thing he or she does several or more times a day with legitimate customers when the opportunity presents itself. The techniques utilized by shopping crews are many and varied in their approach, but all have in common the fact that identification of the questionable transaction can be made by so-called tie-down sales to other members of the shopping

This is a Cash and Production Control form. Properly completed, it gives an accurate record of what has been done in each store. It tells the hours worked by individuals in a crew and an accounting of the shopping money issued, spent and returned.

Figure 5.4 Cash and production control form.

investigation team, which are properly recorded on the cash register or written sales receipt.

A typical integrity shopping crew will consist of two or preferably three people. The best shopping crews seem to be made up of full-time shoppers who have developed their art and are very proficient at it. An alternative to a full-time shopping crew would be a nucleus of at least one full-time or lead shopper, supplemented by part-time shoppers. Often, part-time shoppers can be recruited from the ranks of housewives who at one time or another have worked as a member of a full-time shopping crew.

The crew is usually directed by a so-called lead shopper or crew chief who is responsible for dispensing the cash to make the purchases, transporting the team, and working out the routing and schedule. The crew chief will also act as liaison with his or her principal in the agency office or, in the case of in-house investigation, with the retail security manager.

It will normally be up to the agency supervisor or the retail security manager to make arrangements with the crew chief for the storage of the purchases while the particular series of stores are being shopped over a period of days. Ultimately, all of the merchandise is normally turned in to the company for full credit and this is usually handled through a high-ranking member of the controller's staff of the store. In this way, rank-and-file sales personnel are not aware of shopping investigation merchandise being returned for credit.

Figures 5.3 and 5.4 are examples of some of the report forms used by either agency or in-house shopping investigators.

CHAPTER 6

TAILING AND STATIONARY SURVEILLANCE

Moving and stationary surveillance capabilities are required skills for any well-rounded private security operation. Not only are surveillances often necessary to augment inside undercover operations, but often they may represent the only means of building a case against a suspect. Even in the case of street-type undercover work where penetration of a certain location or the roping of a particular individual is indicated, surveillance is almost always a first step.

VEHICLE SURVEILLANCE

The ability to conduct successful moving surveillance with today's varied traffic conditions is an art. Good "tail" men must have the ability to perform successfully in all types of conditions, whether it is expressway driving, downtown traffic conditions, interstate highway travel, or rural county roads. It becomes readily apparent that only expert drivers can master the art of successful vehicular surveillance. Persons who are knowledgeable in this area would agree that the best tail men are often to be found employed as operatives for private detective agencies specializing in marital investigations. Some of these expert drivers are successful in maintaining weeks of tailing of male subjects who have been alerted beforehand to the strong possibility that such a surveillance may exist. Nevertheless, in spite of the evasive maneuvers that may be attempted by the subject who anticipates a surveillance, these tail men are more often successful than not.

For the beginning investigator, training in the art of vehicular surveillance is absolutely necessary. In surveillance work the subject may become "burned," that is, suspicious or aware of the fact that he is under surveillance, without being able to pinpoint any particular agent. When the term "burned" is used in connection with an agent, it is synonymous with being "made" or identified by the

71

subject. In this case, the agent's usefulness on the assignment in question is at an end.

As many evasive tactics as there are to throw off a surveillance, there is an equal number of tactics that can be employed to reduce the chances of "burning" the subject of the tail. As many of these tactics as possible should be demonstrated to the beginner, and from there his own imagination and experience at this type of work will further expand his abilities. Such training is not unlike the defensive driving courses taught by some of the major automobile insurance companies. Because the scope of this text does not permit an extensive discussion of vehicular tactics, we will confine our consideration to general points that must be borne in mind by the director of any surveillance operation.

The Surveillance Vehicle and Equipment

Rental cars are generally considered to be the best choice for vehicle surveillance. For a surveillance involving more than one person per vehicle, a four-door sedan is preferable to a two-door, as the passenger can often utilize the rear seat to enable a different "picture" to be presented to the subject of the surveillance. By lying prone in the rear seat, the passenger gives a "picture" of a one occupant car, which can later be changed to a two occupant "picture." The vehicle should be chosen carefully so that it is not a conspicuous color. On surveillances running a number of days, cars should be switched with the rental agency on a daily basis if at all possible. Some rental agencies will be amenable to maintaining a weekly rate in spite of the daily changes of automobiles, especially if full-sized sedans are being used.

Items kept in the surveillance vehicle should include changes of outer clothing such as caps, hats, and a reversible jacket or topcoat. Surveillance cars should also contain a pair of good-quality binoculars as well as a motion picture or still camera equipped with telephoto lens. A closed container for liquids is necessary for relief of personal needs during car surveillances that will run an indefinite number of hours. A newspaper should be on hand in the vehicle to enable the operative to have cover for camera work and also to provide a cover for himself when in a parked position. A person sitting in an automobile appearing to read a newspaper draws far less attention than someone who appears to be doing nothing except sitting.

Some agencies of the federal government, along with private agencies that utilize automobiles regularly for tail jobs, have made certain modifications in the automobiles' lights. For instance, by the use of interior switches, either the left or the right headlight can be shut off, or, on the other hand, both lights can be kept turned on. These various combinations, of course, add to the number of different "pictures" presented for the subject's rearview mirror. Interior lights should also be modified to the extent of taping down the spring buttons found in the door panels so that the lights do not come on when the doors are opened. A good investigator should never remove the bulb from the interior dome light; the dome light must be kept in operating condition, for reasons explained later in this chapter.

Risks in Automobile Surveillance

In training the new agent, considerable time should be spent in attempting to inculcate an understanding of when it is permissible to take chances and when it is not. Any successful automobile sur-veillance of necessity involves a certain amount of risk to passengers of the car, pedestrians, and other vehicles on the street. These risks are further increased when it becomes necessary to violate traffic laws, such as running stop signs and red lights or excessive speeding. On a long-term tailing assignment, it may be highly desirable to minimize taking such chances, even though the chances of losing the subject are thereby increased. It is probably reasonable to state that maximum traffic violations are permissible only in the event that the agent knows the "buy" has occurred or is about to take place, or that contraband is being transported to a specific location. Only at a time like this can it be justifiably said that it is not affordable to lose the tail.

Multiple-Auto Surveillance

Obviously, the most difficult car tails are those that involve subjects who own powerful automobiles or are high-speed drivers. The high-speed driver alone is enough of a hazard on the road, and for this reason the surveillance director has to exercise prudent judgment on how a successful tail job can be accomplished. For the successful tailing of such a subject, multiple automobiles must be used—a min-imum of two and possibly three or four, all with adequate radio communication. This can involve a strategy of several of the cars leapfrogging with the subject, running parallel streets, or even a combination of both plus other strategies that can be employed. In attempting to determine a regular route of travel of such a high-speed driver, it may be prudent for the director to utilize a number of days of surveillance, forfeiting the loss of the subject's car each day but at the same time gaining additional distance information on the subject's regular route of travel.

For the department or agency that engages in a heavy volume of vehicular surveillances, there are now devices on the market that can be attached beforehand to the subject vehicle to emit a radio signal. This, of course, requires a combination receiver and direction finder in one of the tail vehicles. The small "beeper" device is easily planted on a target vehicle and becomes extremely useful when visual contact with the vehicle has been lost. The one possible disadvantage to this device is the fact that the transmitter may be lost through heavy jarring in traffic or even discovered by the driver or garage personnel. The obvious financial loss entailed by losing many of these transmitters can easily be seen to be a deterrent to using this method.

Truck Tails

Generally speaking, truck tails are much easier than automobile tails and in corporate security work are probably the more prevalent of the two. Because of their size and unusual markings, trucks are much easier to keep in sight than are automobiles. One thing that the beginning agent must be aware of is the large sideview mirrors that are used with regularity by all truck drivers. For instance, in making a right angle turn, the tail car should always make a much wider turn in order to keep out of view of the particular sideview mirror the truck driver will be using. On the other hand, because sideview mirrors represent the only means of viewing to the rear for the truck driver, there is also an advantage the agent can take. This advantage lies in a visual dead spot immediately behind the truck, out of view of both of the sideview mirrors. This of course involves tailgating the truck, and a high degree of driver capability is required to avoid an accident. However, in heavy downtown traffic conditions this often represents the only method that can be used to stay with the truck at various intersections and through traffic signals.

In corporate security work, most truck surveillances are of company trucks that are regularly making deliveries or pickups. Accordingly, these trucks generally follow a prescribed route, and it is often possible on any given day to be able to determine beforehand which stops are to be made by the driver. Often the surveillance agent will make a dry run of the route beforehand to learn of traffic conditions, special turns, bridges, turn-offs, etc. In making the dry run, the agent also has the opportunity to spot various locations along the route he will recognize as being places that can be used in his own tactics to minimize his exposure to a "burn."

"Burning" the Subject

In both car and truck tails, one of the biggest problems the new agent must overcome is that of mental attitudes. All tail men would readily agree that early in their career they experienced the feeling that they had "burned" the subject and that the subject was aware of the tail. Experience has shown, however, that this suspicion is usually unfounded and the subject has not in fact been "burned." In case after case, experienced tail men will point out that even though they had become convinced that the subject was aware of the tail, later interrogation brought out the fact that he was never aware of being followed. Only the director of a surveillance operation can keep this phenomenon in balance and be able to temper the agent's mental attitude.

As a rule of thumb, the subject who is actually "burned" will usually resort to illogical or seemingly pointless driving tactics in order to confirm in his own mind the probability of a tail. It is at this point that the agent must drop the tail immediately. The very dropping of the tail will confuse the subject further, as he is unable to confirm his initial suspicion. If the tail is not dropped, then the next logical maneuver on the part of the suspect would be evasive driving tactics that would tend to "lose" the tail.

FOOT TAILS

Unlike vehicular tails, which must constantly consider the "picture" being presented to a rearview mirror, foot tails are more concerned with simply keeping the subject in sight and using good common sense so as not to "burn" the case.

In a foot tail, the agent must be prepared for almost any contingency. He should always have ample change in his pocket for the purchase of a newspaper or magazine and making phone calls. Also, he must possess sufficient funds in the event he must use public transportation or travel by taxi. Changes of appearance are also desirable on foot tails, probably even more so than in an automobile tail, as the agent is in the open and more exposed. Here again, a cap, a collapsible hat that can be placed in a pocket, reversible top coat, sunglasses or other eyeglasses, are all props that can greatly aid the agent in maintaining his cover. More traditional disguises, such as false beards, mustaches, and wigs, generally should not be adopted unless the agent is an expert in their use and the items are of excellent quality that will present a real-life appearance.

In teaching beginning agents how to conduct foot tails, one of the tactics that can be employed is the traditional "picking a spot" on the rear of the subject and concentrating on that spot when following in crowded conditions. Reflections in storefront windows can also be used, but at the same time the agent should be aware that an astute subject who suspects a tail will also utilize the same window angles and reflections to confirm his suspicions.

Another tactic used by suspicious subjects is that of "rounding," which simply means making an abrupt U-turn on the sidewalk and retracing one's steps. The purpose of this, of course, is to attempt to confirm the existence of a tail. In such an event, the agent has little choice but to continue straight ahead, at least until the opportunity presents itself to turn a corner or to enter a store as a shopper would. In any event, during such a "rounding" operation, or on a public conveyance, or at any other time, the agent should *always* avoid eye contact with the subject. For some reason, eye contact more than anything else will tend to confirm the existence of a tail in the subject's mind.

STATIONARY SURVEILLANCE

Hotel Surveillance

Hotel surveillances are probably among the most difficult to maintain successfully. Larger hotels give more cover for the agents, but on the other hand also make it more difficult to locate the subject. Smaller hotels, conversely, offer little or no cover for the agent but do make it easier to spot the subject. If the subject is not known to the agents by sight, then obviously they must work with a photograph. Since the subject's appearance may have changed since the photo was taken, the task may seem almost impossible.

The attitude of most first-class hotels is one of noncooperation in the surveillance of their guests. However, it is often possible for the director of such a surveillance, utilizing personal friendships and contacts, to at least gain the passive cooperation of the hotel security chief. By "passive cooperation" we mean that the agents themselves will not be harassed by the hotel security staff even though the security staff does nothing to aid the agents in their work.

On rare occasions, it may be possible for agents to rent a room directly across the hall or at either side of the subject's room. In this way, the job becomes much easier. Utilizing radio communication, the agents are then in a position to become aware of the comings and goings of the subject and to pick up on the street surveillance at the hotel entrance. If it is not possible to gain access to a nearby room, the agents can only resort to frequent trips past the subject's room, listening for sounds (or the lack thereof) from within the room, and "plugging" the door. "Plugging" the door means the insertion in the door jamb of a match, toothpick, thread, or other small inconspicuous item that will drop from place when the door is opened.

Use of Vans, Campers, and Buildings

Setting up a surveillance in a business district is usually an easy matter. Even if parking considerations are a problem, the initial point of contact can be handled by one agent on foot with radio communication to the back-up surveillance. In a residential neighborhood, the point of pick-up for the surveillance team can become a problem. Not only are neighbors apt to become alarmed and call the police at the sight of a strange vehicle parked in a residential neighborhood; they may very well become suspicious to the point that loose conversation will eventually find its way to the suspect and alert him to the surveillance.

If an automobile must be utilized in a residential neighborhood, then the surveillance director may decide that he will have to accept the possibility of suspicion on the part of the neighbors. But at least he can attempt to divert the direction of that suspicion. For example, the common tendency is to suspect that the location being watched is in front of the surveillance vehicle, in the direction towards which the agent or agents appear to be facing. In other words, the surveillance director can present this type of a "picture" to neighborhood residents, when in fact the agents are watching a pick-up point to the rear of the surveillance vehicle via the use of sideview and/or rearview mirrors.

One complication that has arisen in recent years for surveillance of residential neighborhoods is the fact that many communities have introduced a neighborhood Crime Watch Program. The Crime Watch Program makes it extremely difficult to surveil from an automobile even though the police may have been alerted. Regardless of a police promise of cooperation, the police are obligated to respond to a telephone call where a neighborhood Crime Watch Program is in effect and to check out the occupants of a vehicle.

The optimum solution to residential surveillance is the use of a surveillance van or camper-type vehicle. After a day or two, such a vehicle parked in a residential neighborhood draws absolutely no attention. Most of the neighbors conclude that it belongs to some visiting friends or relatives of a local resident. The use of well-equipped surveillance vans has gained in popularity in recent years, especially in corporate security departments. One large mail order house with numerous retail outlets across the country is reported to have about fifteen of these vehicles in use. Although vans are gen-

erally not desirable for a moving surveillance, especially of automobiles, they seem to be the perfect answer to the need for cover on
a stationary surveillance. Campers easily serve the same purpose,
the only drawback is that there is generally no direct means of access
from the inside of the camper to the cab of the truck.

In some business districts, where a long-term stationary surveillance is desirable, it is often possible to take an informal rental
of a small store building or an unused office. Most rental agents will
often agree to the temporary rental of such a unit, especially where
the transaction is handled by cash. In this type of situation, the
security agent must be alert to the possibility that the rental agency
may show the premises for possible legitimate leasing. The surveillance agent's furnishings, therefore, should be kept to an absolute
minimum.

The use of a proper cover for a stationary foot surveillance,
such as would be maintained during a "buy," is limited only by
one's imagination. Here, the cover could easily take the form of a
small construction project, street cleaners, taxicab drivers, fishermen
at a dockside, sidewalk distributors of leaflets or flyers, or any other
suitable arrangement.

Coordination With Police

The question of how far to bring the local police into a private investigation can be a thorny one indeed.

The problem arises because the police, in their efforts to do a
proper job of patrolling, are bound to come into contact with stationary surveillance teams or may simply respond to telephone complaints from local residents. Under no circumstances should members
of a surveillance team ever reveal to squad car personnel the target
of their surveillance. Normally, it should be sufficient for the agents
to identify themselves and state the fact that they are on a surveillance but are not at liberty to reveal the person against whom the
surveillance is directed. In some small rural communities it may be
advisable for the investigator not to show any official identification
but to present, instead, his driver's license and attempt to utilize a
pretext story that may satisfy the responding police patrolman.

If the security executive decides initially that the local chief or
other high-ranking police official can be trusted, then an arrangement
might be worked out whereby the surveillance members simply state
to the responding patrolman, "We are on a special project, with
which Chief Jones is thoroughly familiar." This, of course, is not
completely satisfying to the patrolman, but on the other hand he
usually will think twice before challenging that type of statement
when it implies that his own chief is privy to the situation.

One of the problems that comes about through the activities of the police patrol is the fact that in stopping the surveillance agents, the police view them as suspicious persons who are loitering in the area and may require them to get out of the vehicle and undergo a search. They may even call for an additional back-up unit with the intention of removing the agents from the area to police headquarters for further questioning. All of this activity tends to attract the attention of neighbors in the community and, of course, that makes it impossible to use that location again.

Agents who are conducting stationary surveillance from inside a van should be instructed to never open the van regardless of any police order. It is common practice for a responding police patrolman to approach the van and order the occupant out. However, it must be kept in mind that even the police officer does not know for sure that there is someone in the van and to respond to such an order would only confirm to all of the watching neighbors that, indeed, the van is occupied. In many cases, officers may even beat on the van with their night sticks ordering the operative to emerge, but the best advice that can be given is for the agent to lie on the floor and be calm. If the police department should take it upon itself to tow the van away from the area, then, of course, the operative will have to make his presence known but, hopefully, the van may be hooked up and towed away to another location before the agent is forced to actually show himself. Again, the agent should be instructed that if he has done his job properly, there is no way the police officer can be certain that he is in the van and, for that reason, he should not respond to an order to emerge.

In many cases, there will be a back-up car that can be summoned by radio by the agent in the interior of the van. The back-up car agent should be able to dissuade the police officers from damaging the van or towing it away.

In a large police department, prior arrangements can sometimes be made through a high-ranking commanding officer so that instructions can be issued to the patrolmen on the beat that a surveillance car with private agents is going to be positioned in the area of a particular block. The block so designated may not be the target of the surveillance itself but an adjoining block; even though a certain amount of suspicion is created on the part of the local residents, it will not be apt to filter back to the suspect.

Experience has shown that when agents are stopped by a police car for speeding, upon displaying proper credentials and explaining to the officer that they are on a tail job involving a larceny, in most cases they will be allowed to proceed without a citation being issued. Here again, the agents should not reveal the type of vehicle being tailed, for there is really no need for this; if the officer presses for this information, it is only because of personal curiosity.

If the surveillance agents are on a stationary stake-out of a particular location and they are approached at night by a police officer, their first act should be to turn on the interior lights of the car. Most policemen are extremely wary of approaching one or more occupants in a parked car at night and usually do so only when they have unholstered their weapons or at least removed the safety snap from the holster. The sudden appearance of an interior light in the automobile tends to reduce the anxiety of the approaching officer and conveys the message that the agents are legitimate and that everything is open and aboveboard.

Communications and Special Equipment

Coordinating with either inside or street undercover agents, the tail men should work out in advance a contact point whereby messages can be relayed via telephone. Often the undercover agent may become aware of last-minute changes in the suspects' planning, and unless a prearranged line of communication is set up, he will be unable to convey this information to the surveillance agents. The undercover agent may also be necessary to identify or to "finger" certain suspects in the case. This, of course, has to be worked out in advance with the surveillance personnel so that they can "pick up" the suspect. (As used in surveillance work, the term "pick up" is not to be confused with its use as a synonym for apprehension. It simply denotes the beginning of a tail job of a particular subject at a specific location.)

Prior to the advent of modern-day radio equipment, hand signals were often the only way to accomplish the leapfrog concept of multiple-vehicle surveillance. Today, nationwide companies are able to obtain a designated frequency for the use of UHF radio equipment. A good radio communication consultant is really the key to the solution of radio problems and their legality anywhere in the country. One major corporation has been able to secure a radio license covering every major location point within its industrial complex in the United States. This enables its corporate security department to move from locale to locale and still use its UHF radio equipment legally.

Earlier, reference was made to the use of a specially equipped surveillance van. A number of security departments have purchased stock vans from major auto manufacturers and modified them for their own use. If such a van is to be disguised in some way, then proper consideration should be given to the van's "cover." For example, the van may have signs describing it as belonging to an industrial testing company, an engineering survey company, a pollution study firm, etc. If such cover is utilized and signs are affixed to the

Figure 6.1   Disguised in an air vent, the periscope enables occupants of surveillance van to observe subjects without detection.

van, then the cover should be complete with telephone numbers that at least answer and identify themselves as an answering service.

The interior of the van should be pretty much tailor-made to the needs of the operation, but at least should contain proper camera equipment, binoculars, chemical toilet, and food and beverage storage to enable the agent to remain in the van for at least several days. Obviously, this predicates equipping the van with at least a folding cot, a small table for writing reports, and other emergency equipment.

An innovation that has been made available for surveillance vans is a type of periscope that enables the occupants of the van not only to observe their target but also to make use of their photographic equipment through the periscope (see Figure 6.1). Lacking a periscope, the van can be rigged with black-out curtains on all of the windows with the exception of the window being utilized for observation. This reverse lighting effect enables the occupant to view outward through a curtain of linen composition but makes it virtually impossible for someone on the outside to be able to view the interior of the van.

Conclusion

Obviously, not every case lends itself to successful conclusion through the use of the various surveillance techniques. On the other hand, there is always a certain percentage of cases that can be completed in a proper fashion only through stakeouts and surveillance. A command of the intricacies of the art of surveillance is an indication of the overall ability of the security executive.

CHAPTER 7

SUPPLEMENTARY
INVESTIGATIVE METHODS

Many cases are of such a nature that neither undercover work nor various forms of surveillance are appropriate investigative approaches. In other cases these approaches fail to produce the necessary information to conclude the matter. This would be especially true of high-level executive crime, where undercover investigation would be totally out of the question and various surveillance attempts would probably produce only limited results. In these types of situations, the investigation manager must turn to other avenues of information to develop a case.

Agency Background Checks

In the case of investigative subjects with interstate backgrounds, a good starting point might be a background investigation conducted by a national agency specializing in this type of work. A number of good agencies perform this service. Agencies of this type are able to pool various investigative requests into certain geographical areas, resulting in a savings to the client, unless a priority is requested so that all investigative effort is directed to a single request. These agencies have investigators who regularly spend parts of each working week in courthouses and in close contact with various credit bureaus, and also have occasional regular contact with educational institutions and the like. The use of such an investigation agency is a great time- and money-saver to the investigations manager. It will provide at least an overview of the subject's background and may very well indicate leads of questionable areas that should be pursued in a follow-up investigation.

Most background investigations of the type mentioned above cost a minimum of $350 and may cost as much as one to two thousand dollars, depending on the information requested and the number of geographical points and contacts that must be made. The important thing to be remembered in using this approach is that most of the information is obtained through direct personal contact. There is little use of mail or telephone, as there is by some agencies offering background investigations in the neighborhood of fifty to one hundred dollars. Anyone experienced in background investigations will readily appreciate the advantage of spending the extra money to obtain the personal interview of past employers and credit sources, rather than using the faceless approach of the mails and telephone.

In addition to agencies specializing in standard background-type investigation, other agencies have developed expertise in tracking public information records. One agency in particular[7] has become so proficient in digging out information that is public in nature that it has been retained by a number of federal agencies including the FBI, the DEA, and the IRS to perform background searches on a contract basis. Federal agencies certainly have personnel who are capable of performing this task, but the time involved to become really sophisticated at this work is probably prohibitive and therefore this type of work is occasionally "farmed out."

This same agency mentioned above operates a school for training law enforcement officials and corporate security personnel and other security types.[8] It is referred to as a Public Information Records Tracking (P.I.R.T.) agency. As a point of interest, the school brochure listing of services is shown in Table 7.1.

In-House Supplemental Investigation

After receiving the results of a nationwide background investigation, such as described above, the security manager is often able to zero in on loose ends that need to be followed up or even leads or questionable areas that may have been developed by the original investigative agency. These follow-up investigations are often more productive when performed by the security manager or his staff. This is especially true when it comes to a high-level interview that is conducted with a top-ranking executive in another corporation. Experience has shown that often a corporate executive will be inclined to be more candid with a corporate security person than with the representative of the security agency who conducted the initial check. Corporate executives may be less than candid when talking to an agency investigator because of fear of libel or slander suits.

In summary, the background investigative agency can usually

---

[7]International Intelligence Network Corp., PO Box 42999/Department 117, Houston, Texas 77042.
[8]*Ibid.*

Table 7.1 Intelligence Information That May Be tained from a Completed Public Records Search

Full Name	Present/Past Banks, S&L's, C.D.'s, Officer's Name	Capitalization
Alias, A/K/A, D/B/A	Trust, Beneficiary, Donor, Trustee	Subsidiaries or Parent Corporations
Date of Birth	Inheritances	Limited Partnerships
Place of Birth	Sale of Assets	Tax Liens, Date and Type of Tax
Citizenship	Loans & Collateral	Security Exchange 10K Filings
Parents Name	Mortgages	Accountants or C.P.A. Names
Residence Address	Damages from Litigation	Attorneys That Do or Have Represented Subject
Phone Number	Mortgage Receivables	Dates, Case, Cause #, Court, Location
Business	Automobiles	Number of Cases as Defendant and Brief of Cases
Business Address	Equipment	Number of Cases as Plaintiff and Brief of Cases
Business Phone Number	Real Estate	Trustees Acting For, Name and Date, Film Code #s, Location
Additional Present or Prior Addresses	Airplanes	Inventories of Estates, Probate
Marital Status	Boats	Wills
Date and Place of Marriage	Loans	Liquor License
Spouses' Maiden Name	Assets Purchased by Financing	Bank Stocks Owned
Spouses' Parents' Names	Business by D/B/A	Bankruptcy
Children's Names	Corporations	Criminal Records Via Court Records
Occupation	Present Corporate Address	Associates
Length of Time at Present Occupation	Charter Number	Newspaper Records
Prior Occupations	Charter Date	Immigration Information
Spouses' Occupation	Charter Standing	Property Tax Value
Education and Civic Associations	Registered Agent	
Military Service	Registered Address	Combinations of the Preceding Items and Multiples of Lead Information Germane to Your End Result Requirement.
Social Security Number & State of Issue	Incorporators	
	Officers & Directors	

act as a tremendous time- and money-saver to the security manager by simultaneously working investigative or background leads in various parts of the country. This approach enables the security manager to make an intelligent decision regarding the area or locale on which he will focus his own in-house effort.

Bribery and Kickback Cases

To most corporate security managers, the most difficult and frustrating cases to bring to a successful conclusion are bribery and kickback cases. In many industries, bribery or kickbacks are a way of life, something that is taken for granted by executives in that particular industry.

Company Policy. Some companies attempt to dampen the kickback problem through the use of periodic written communications to their suppliers. These communications generally state the company's policy as to honest business practices, suggest tactfully to the supplier that kickbacks are unnecessary to do business, and advise the supplier that if kickbacks are solicited by a particular executive, they should be reported. Coincident with this, many of these same companies will make use of a conflict-of-interest questionnaire that must be completed and signed annually by all key executive personnel.

Such deterrents may serve well in the case of a basically honest executive who might otherwise be tempted. On the other hand, they are of little value to the corporation with a dishonest executive who has been solicited by a dishonest supplier to engage in a kickback arrangement.

Difficulty of Detection. There are statutes at the state and federal levels covering bribery and kickback situations involving public servants in their relationships with outside contractors or service companies. Most of these laws contain serious penalties for conviction and are on a felony level. For executives of private companies, however, it is generally not illegal to engage in such behavior. Only a few states have seen fit to pass commercial bribery statutes. However, virtually all of these are classified as misdemeanors and in reality would probably draw absolutely no jail time whatsoever.

The truth of the matter is that unless either the "bribee" or the "briber" decides to reveal the existence of such a practice, the kickback scheme may very well go undetected; even if suspected, it may be impossible to prove. Some of these kickback cases have been brought to light by a close business associate who was not involved but who knew of the scheme. However, in virtually all of the situations, the company executive who was the kickback recipient was a long-term employee with much to lose by admitting to the scheme. Unless there is a falling-out between the two participants and one comes forward and makes such an admission, the only other approach that can be used is interrogation. Interrogation should be undertaken only after as many facts as possible have been developed through ordinary investigative methods.

As an example of how interrogation might be productive after suitable investigation, we present the following case history:

Los Angeles, California. The president of a large Southern California retail store chain was suspected of taking kickbacks from clothing vendors. The kickbacks apparently came in the form of both cash and men's clothing that were routinely delivered to his office and then carried home after several days. The original informant was a company secretary who was loyal to the corporate office.

No hard evidence beyond the allegations of the secretary could be obtained and therefore it was decided to put the executive under surveillance during a buying trip to New York City. The buying trip lasted approximately four days, with the president arriving in the city of New York on a Sunday evening. He was immediately placed under surveillance and the surveillance was maintained throughout all of his waking hours until he once again departed for California on Thursday evening. During this time, he was wined and dined and entertained by a number of New York vendors who customarily picked up the luncheon and dinner checks in the various restaurants in which they ate. One thing the surveillance crew noticed was that the executive would often obtain unused dinner checks from the cashier upon leaving various restaurants.

Upon his return to California, an expense report came in from the retail president to corporate headquarters listing his entertainment for the week. For the most part, the entertainment and meals were documented with receipts attached to the expense report. An investigator was assigned to check out the receipts and make contact with the various owners of the restaurants listed on the report. Out of approximately ten receipts that were submitted, five restaurants were willing to cooperate and stated that the meal checks were out of sequence for the period of time involved and the handwriting on the receipts did not correspond with any known samples of restaurant personnel.

Armed with these incontrovertible facts, an interrogation in Los Angeles was begun that successfully proved not only the padding of the expense report but also the receipt of thousands of dollars worth of clothing from vendors as part of a regular kickback scheme. The retail president's employment was terminated forthwith.

Outside Agency Investigation. Here again, as with background investigations, a personal investigation of the suspected recipient can be conducted by an outside agency. This is generally preferable to an in-house approach, because in any investigation of this type there is always a certain risk that the subject of the investigation will learn of the investigative efforts. By employing an outside agency, the security manager at least sets up a layer of insulation between himself and his co-executive who is being investigated.

Even when utilizing an outside agency, the security manager should exercise close control over the investigation and make the decisions about what investigative sources will be checked and what persons will be interviewed by the agency. A surveillance of the suspect may prove beneficial, along with a covert inspection of his business quarters after hours. In some cases, the security manager may be able to use personal contacts he has developed with his counterparts in various stores and utility agencies to obtain information relating to current accounts, long distance telephone calls, and other useful information.

Internal Auditing Department. Another useful approach in attempting to develop investigative leads is through the use of the internal auditing department. It is generally expected by most executives that internal auditors perform periodic routine examinations of certain business records and financial information. To make use of this ploy for a specific examination of a suspect's company accounts is an excellent pretext. The auditor is often able to come up with additional leads through an examination of the suspect's expense reports, travel records, etc. Even if the security manager wishes to make the examinations himself, the auditor is in a much better position than a security representative to secure such documents without arousing suspicion.

Recipient's Own Records. In kickback cases, the recipient almost always keeps an independent record of the goods purchased and the margin of kickback that is applied. This may take the form of a small diary kept in his desk, loose sheets of paper in a folder, or a three-ring loose-leaf notebook kept in the trunk of the recipient's car. Through the use of his own resourcefulness, ingenuity, and imagination, the security manager will occasionally be able to conclude a kickback case successfully.

Company Morality. It has been the author's experience in many years of corporate security work that in companies that have a high degree of morality in upper management, kickbacks and bribery cases are usually at a minimum. On the other hand, where the chief executive officer of the corporation does not set a proper moral tone for the company, it seems that white collar crime is much more rampant than would otherwise be found.

Although it does not directly address problems of kickbacks and other forms of dishonesty, one company's moral credo is presented in Figure 7.1 showing the moral atmosphere within that corporation.

Interviews With Witnesses

As the typical investigative case nears its culmination, the security manager may be tempted to resort to interviews with witnesses in order to strengthen the facts already obtained. As one can surmise, overt interviews with witnesses are usually more productive than interviews by pretext. By the same token, they are also riskier than pretext interviews. In most companies today, there is still a small cadre of employees who possess a loyalty to the company transcending any loyalty to their fellow workers. It is these people who are often more susceptible to overt interviews than any others. The basic company loyalty of such persons is only enhanced by an open, direct interview with a top security representative. It should be kept in mind that this is an experience that most employees never encounter, and many witnesses actually feel flattered that the security department of a large corporation would seek them out and spend time with them as witnesses during an interview.

With other types of employees or with outsiders, an interview by pretext is often the only safe approach. Security representatives must be familiar with the laws of the state in which they are operating to insure that there is no prohibition against interviews by pretext. Some common pretext approaches are insurance risk investigations, job applicant or background investigations, consumer and demographic surveys, and poll-taking. Here again, the approach to be used is only limited by one's imagination and whatever legal restrictions apply.

The timing of such interviews, whether overt or by pretext, is all-important. There are risks involved in both approaches, and the security manager must weigh these risks against what there is to be gained. The risks are often minimized by a very close tie-in between the interview and the actual breaking of the case itself. In these instances the interview may very well be worthwhile. The following case example illustrates this point:

New York, New York. Based on information received from an informant, the security manager of a large national company realized the existence of a kickback scheme in the sales department. Basically, sales trainees were required to pay "tribute" to their supervisor, who, after taking his cut, passed the remainder on to the regional sales manager and to the national sales manager. The money was generated by falsifying travel expense reports under the guidance of the ter-

Our Credo

We believe our first responsibility is to the doctors, nurses and patients,
to mothers and fathers and all others who use our products and services.
In meeting their needs everything we do must be of high quality.
We must constantly strive to reduce our costs
in order to maintain reasonable prices.
Customers' orders must be serviced promptly and accurately.
Our suppliers and distributors must have an opportunity
to make a fair profit.

We are responsible to our employees,
the men and women who work with us throughout the world.
Everyone must be considered as an individual.
We must respect their dignity and recognize their merit.
They must have a sense of security in their jobs.
Compensation must be fair and adequate,
and working conditions clean, orderly and safe.
We must be mindful of ways to help our employees fulfill
their family responsibilities.
Employees must feel free to make suggestions and complaints.
There must be equal opportunity for employment, development
and advancement for those qualified.
We must provide competent management,
and their actions must be just and ethical.

We are responsible to the communities in which we live and work
and to the world community as well.
We must be good citizens — support good works and charities
and bear our fair share of taxes.
We must encourage civic improvements and better health and education.
We must maintain in good order
the property we are privileged to use,
protecting the environment and natural resources.

Our final responsibility is to our stockholders.
Business must make a sound profit.
We must experiment with new ideas.
Research must be carried on, innovative programs developed
and mistakes paid for.
New equipment must be purchased, new facilities provided
and new products launched.
Reserves must be created to provide for adverse times.
When we operate according to these principles,
the stockholders should realize a fair return.

Johnson & Johnson

Figure 7.1   One company's moral credo. (Courtesy of Johnson & Johnson, New Brunswick, New Jersey, U.S.A.)

ritory salesmen. The trainees were allowed to keep half of any excess funds, so that they, too, quickly became compromised. For years this particular sales region had been used as a training ground for the rest of the country.

It was decided to interview initially all former trainees who had left the company, just prior to interrogating the two top executives. In order to maintain the element of surprise, key security representatives left New York on a Friday evening, fanning out across the country. Over Saturday and Sunday, former trainees were interviewed in such diverse places as Atlanta, Oklahoma City, Dallas, Los Angeles, Chicago, and many other cities. Signed statements were obtained from virtually all of them and the interviewers were back in New York by Monday morning. On that day in question, both executives were intercepted for interrogation as they arrived for work. Later events confirmed that only one executive had been forewarned, and this only by a single phone call that was very general in nature and had not revealed any specific admissions.

The value of a thorough interview should never be discounted. It should be kept in mind that among the most successful skip tracers in the country today, good interviews constitute probably fifty percent of the successful techniques utilized. (A skip tracer is an investigator who specializes in locating persons who have "skipped"— that is, absconded to avoid payment of debts or other obligations.)

Covert Facility Inspections

Unlike overt inspections of company facilities, which are intended to act as a deterrent to business crime, the covert facility inspection is designed to develop evidence without alerting the suspects. Common sense dictates that such inspections of business facilities should always be conducted after hours when the likelihood of discovery is at an absolute minimum. Here again, the investigator is looking for corroborating evidence that can be found in personal records, diaries, desk calendars, etc. In the case of non-executive personnel in a factory or distribution center facility, the investigator can easily look for contraband in lockers, caches of merchandise in work stations or out-of-the-way locations, narcotics or dangerous drugs, gambling paraphernalia, or anything else that would assist an interrogator in overcoming the resistance of a suspect and obtaining a written confession.

SECTION III

The "Bust": Closing the Investigation

CHAPTER 8

PREPARATIONS FOR THE "BUST"

Having discussed in Section I the various indicators of theft in the business or industrial setting, and in Section II the investigative methods used to further pursue these indicators, we arrive at a cross-roads faced by many companies when the probability of extensive internal theft suddenly becomes a certainty and a reality. Top management must decide whether entrenched thieves should be rooted out; whether only one or two should be singled out as an example; or whether added controls and restraints should be implemented within the company to make it more difficult for the thieving to continue.

Many veteran security chiefs have come to the conclusion that added controls and restraints are intended for workers who are basically honest but might otherwise be tempted by loose procedures and an immoral plant atmosphere. They further believe that employees who have developed such patterns of theft as to be classified as professional or semi-professional thieves cannot be easily rehabilitated or even deterred by added controls. In these cases the only solution is to identify the thieves, separate them from the company payroll, and, where possible, prosecute.

Experience has shown that many corporate security managers and directors of investigative agencies are extremely reluctant to tackle large theft groups in a company facility. Many security heads have not had the experience or even the opportunity to close up a case involving large numbers of confirmed thieves. Accordingly, Section III of this text will emphasize the techniques necessary in handling a large organized theft group, as opposed to more conventional methods that might be used with one or two employee thieves. The successful techniques that will be discussed have evolved over a period of time and are both proven and flexible, capable of meeting changing and different conditions. The plan of action to be developed in the following chapters will work each and every time, if the security chief has the authority, intestinal fortitude, and ability to carry out the detailed planning that are necessarily part of the case.

Admittedly, some of these concepts can be classified as a radical approach, but they can be likened to radical surgery for cancer. Many authorities have come to view widespread theft in industry as an industrial cancer, and in a union shop the "surgeon" or security chief must realize that he probably will get one shot at the disease and one shot only. In the author's experience, the concepts that follow have proved successful in 64 out of 65 attempts—successful in that signed statements or other evidence sufficient to sustain discharge were obtained from a majority of the suspects. In the only failure experienced, the scene of action was outside the United States and the closing of the investigation was made impossible because of strong nationalistic feelings on the part of the perpetrators.

Picking the Date and Time

The planning involved in an operation seeking to close a case on a group of ten to twenty or more hard-core thieving employees can be likened to the planning required for a military operation. Where large numbers of suspects are involved, the "bust" will always have some effect on the day-to-day operations of the company, and for this reason top management must be in agreement on what is the least disruptive date from a production standpoint. In order to permit peak shipping schedules to be met, for example, the date chosen might be as much as thirty days beyond the closing investigatory days of the case.

From the security chief's standpoint, the day of the week on which the closing operation begins is extremely important. The case must move rapidly and be concluded before the end of the normal work week. Therefore, a Monday is highly desirable; certainly a closing should be commenced no later in the week than Tuesday if large numbers of people must be dealt with. The time of day is also extremely important. The investigators must be able to utilize as much of the normal work day as possible for their closing operation, as it is often difficult to operate on an overtime basis beyond the plant's normal quitting time.

Need for Detailed Planning

In planning for the closing of a large-scale internal theft investigation, the security chief should view the entire operation as a military-type exercise, with the enemy represented by the hard-core thieves or theft ring. In a militant union situation, the union must also be recognized as a potentially dangerous ally (either willing or unwilling) of the theft group.

Many union locals have long viewed company security departments as "tools of the bosses" and have given security personnel such epithets as "Company Gestapo" or "Company Pigs." Accordingly, during the course of a major investigation or attempts at interrogation of rank-and-file employees, many union locals will immediately jump to the aid of the employees by advising them of their "rights." In the past, some union locals have issued statements to the workers advising them to refuse to talk to security personnel, to refrain from making any admissions or signing any statements, or even to refuse to be interviewed without the shop steward being present. A number of unions have incorporated into their constitutions or bylaws prohibitions against one worker implicating a fellow union member. All of these factors work to the detriment of the security chief and greatly impede an investigation. Officially, virtually all unions take a stance against employee thievery. Realistically, the most that a security director can hope for is that the union local will remain passive throughout the investigation and enable him to complete his task.

With all of the above considerations in mind, it becomes clear that in order for the closing of the investigation to be successful, the planning must be detailed and sufficient in scope to enable the security personnel to excise the cancer before the entrenched thieves or the union have an opportunity to raise defenses against the operation.

Investigation Summary

After picking a time and date for the closing of the investigation, the security director must now summarize and cross-reference all the information that has been developed throughout the investigation. Normally, the bulk of this data will be extracted from undercover reports, but the case file may also very well include the results of successful surveillances, tail jobs, or other investigative efforts.

Most undercover and surveillance reports are written in a chronological order based on date and time. In the investigation summary, pertinent information is extracted according to each suspect and then reassembled in chronological order under each suspect's name. The undercover information can easily be integrated with outside surveillance reports and information from any other sources.

The purpose of the investigation summary is to provide each member of the interrogation team a synopsis of all pertinent information developed on each suspect in the case. As the interrogator ultimately is assigned various suspects for interrogation, he will immediately have at his fingertips every bit of information known about each particular suspect. This gives an interrogator a tremendous advantage and easily accounts for the confession success rates of 90 and 95 percent that are common in investigation closings of this type. Psychologically, the appearance of an investigation summary, which has been typed and may be contained in a folder, is devastating to the suspect. With this type of assistance, a skilled interrogator can completely destroy the psychological defenses normally raised by a suspect in this kind of situation.

In compiling the investigation summary, the security director must be careful not to expose the existence of his undercover agent. Normally, the summary can be written in such a way to make it appear that conversations held with the undercover agent by various suspects were overheard by a third party. In addition, employees can often be led into believing in the existence of hidden microphones and cameras. The suspect can also be advised that evening interviews have been held with certain key employees in their homes and that much of the information has been obtained in this manner. This is based on the premise that many of the employees know about theft taking place in the plant even though they may not be involved themselves.

Realizing that the various interrogators may not appreciate the delicacy of the undercover investigation, the security director must make every effort in writing the summary to conceal the true identity of the undercover investigator. Furthermore, it must also be realized that the investigation summary may ultimately fall into the wrong hands, either inadvertently or through legal process—all the more reason that the identity of the undercover agent must not be compromised. The following are examples of investigation summaries from actual cases.

B_____, Ed
Employed as order filler, 1 year. Subject drives a white Cadillac
12-1   Subject overheard stating to other employees that he had been stealing shirts and placing them in his automobile.
12-14   Subject overheard telling another employee that most of the shirts which he stole were taken out of the building on Saturdays.
1-21   Subject was overheard stating to another employee that he had agreed to steal 30 shirts for L_____ W_____ on this date. However, L_____ did not come to work.
1-22   Subject was overheard stating to another employee that he had a part-time job working at night at the _____ department store in Marietta. He was overheard to state that he had stolen about $500 worth of goods since employed there.
1-27   Subject observed stealing 2 shirts and placing them in his car during lunch period. These were placed under the floor mat,

as per usual. At quitting time, subject observed stealing 4 additional shirts. It is to be noted that subject seems to steal most of the shirts when he wears a blue jacket.

2-2   Subject overheard discussing with another employee the possibility of slipping 3 or 4 additional cases of shirts on the truck which makes a shuttle run between warehouses. The gist of the conversation was that the seal would not be put on tight and that the shirts could be dropped at a location on McAfee Street.

2-4   Subject and another employee were observed slipping an extra case of shirts on the shuttle truck (3-8/12 doz.). Outside surveillance developed the fact that shirts were dropped off at Apt. 620, 5 McAfee Street, Atlanta. After the shirts were dropped off it was noted that B_____ actually locked the seal on the truck. At quitting time on this date subject was observed stealing 2 additional shirts from the warehouse and then selling them to employee L_____ D_____ outside the warehouse.

2-15   Information received that subject may, on occasion, carry a pistol which he has stolen from the _____ store. Subject overheard in conversation this date stating that he had stolen a total of 3 pistols.

Outside surveillance indicated that several extra cases were loaded on the shuttle truck to which subject was assigned at the M_____ warehouse and that these extra cases of shirts were dropped off at the address at McAfee Street. It was noted that subject and another employee returned to the McAfee address after quitting time and apparently made a split of the loot. Subject was also overheard during the day at the warehouse to state that he assisted another employee who worked in the Military section to remove 5 shirts from the warehouse.

H_____, Willie Frank

Terminated approximately 6 weeks ago for tardiness. Drives a sky blue Volkswagen.

10-23   At approximately 1:00 p.m. subject was observed examining the contents of different shirt boxes and at one point was observed placing a shirt down inside his trousers. After leaving the area he returned and repeated the procedure, taking another shirt.

10-26   Subject observed placing 2 shirts in his trousers during the afternoon. It is estimated that at the rate of theft which has been observed that subject may take as many as 20 to 30 shirts during the course of a particular day.

10-27   Subject observed again during the afternoon on this date stealing a large quantity of shirts.

10-29   Subject overheard expressing concern about the removal of a cache of 50 shirts which he had in the warehouse. This resulted from a security meeting held by management for the employees.

11-13   Subject was seen showing a stolen shirt to another employee at quitting time and also was overheard to make the statement that this represented the 9th shirt which he had stolen on this date. Subject was further overheard to state that he wears a girdle to hold the shirts in place. Subject also overheard to implicate Louis _____ in the theft of 9 shirts and that A_____ allegedly also wears a girdle.

11-24   Subject observed in the company of Willie _____, Tony _____ and Johnny _____ stealing a large quantity of shirts and placing them in the pockets of their coats.

11-30   At approximately 4:00 p.m. subject observed placing a shirt inside of his pants. This was witnessed by a picker named Paul _____.

12-16   Subject observed removing 2 shirts from under his trousers and placing them on the back seat of his car at quitting time. This was witnessed by employee Leroy _____.

12-17   Information developed this date which would indicate that subject is working in collusion with employee Leroy _____. Subject was observed removing 4 shirts from his pants and placing same on the back seat of his car. Later, subject stopped at a "drop," which was an old wrecked car, and took out 2 more shirts. These had apparently been placed in the wreck during the noon hours.

12-18   Subject overheard stating to another employee that he had only stolen 4 shirts on this date.

1-4   Subject observed taking 1 shirt on this date and was overheard telling another employee that he had an order to get 25 more shirts by the following Friday for $125. Subject stated that he had anticipated taking most of them during the lunch hour.

1-5   Subject observed stealing 4 shirts on this date.

1-6   Subject observed stealing 4 shirts on this date. Subject was overheard boasting that he was becoming so proficient in theft that he was able to steal shirts without taking off the wrappers.

1-7   Subject observed stealing 2 shirts on this date.

1-8   Subject observed stealing 3 shirts at quitting this date.

1-11   Subject observed in theft of only 1 shirt this date. Subject was overheard telling another employee that he had obtained $130 from the deal which he made the previous Saturday. He further stated that his contact wanted an additional 25 shirts.

1-12   Subject observed in the theft of 2 shirts this date.

H_____, Tom

Subject drives a dark blue Volkswagen which is usually parked near the back fence. License #BB-183.

10-20   Subject overheard announcing at lunch time to the other employees that he had "speed" available for sale.

11-6   Subject believed to have supplied Kenneth _____ with a quantity of "hash" on this date.

11-12   Subject overheard offering to sell either opium or "speed" to another employee.

11-13   At approximately 2:45 p.m. subject was observed selling an unknown quantity of "hash" to another employee for $8. This transaction took place in the men's restroom.

12-16   Subject overheard in the men's restroom offering to sell 70 hits of "speed."

1-11   Subject, along with two other employees, observed in the men's room smoking marijuana. Subject is now believed to be in business with employee Ernest _____ in the selling of drugs and narcotics within the warehouse.

1-29   Subject observed at about quitting time selling 3 capsules of "speed."

2-5   Subject observed selling some "hash" to another employee. Also overheard stating that he was going to attempt to get supervisor Skip S_____ to buy some illicit drugs.

3-3   Subject observed selling "joints."

O_____, Clay

10-28   Employee Jim _____ overheard in conversation that another employee implicated subject in the theft of 3 new large ashtrays the previous night. It was alleged that subject had them under his coat when he went out at quitting time.

10-29   Subject involved in steady drinking on the 3:00 to 11:00 p.m. shift on this date in the company of Jim _____, Roger _____ and others. Subject brags of multiple arrests for drunk and disorderly. After the drinking episode the men re-entered the plant at approximately 10:30 p.m. and subject made a notation on the Tenting machine pad, "Down 9:45 to 11:00 p.m.— Machine overheated." Then subject was observed turning all of the dials on to high, which in fact caused the machine to overheat. Subject also observed punching out Roger _____'s time card this date.

11-7   Subject engaged in heavy drinking on this date. (See entry on William _____). While intoxicated, subject stated that he had murdered his Sergeant while in Vietnam by shooting him in the back of the head while on patrol. He also admitted that he had had apparent psychiatric problems in connection with his military experience.

11-12   Subject overheard in conversation with other employees admitting that he had taken home a whole box of masking tape.

11-17   Subject was overheard this date telling another employee how he causes false readings on the Totalizer by hitting it and causing the numbers to jump as much as 1,000 yards each time.

11-25   Subject believed to have been picked up by the Saratoga police at the plant on this date. (To be verified later.)

11-30   Subject participated in a theft and drinking orgy on this date along with others. He was directly involved in theft of a can of Babo, allegedly intended for William _____, a tape measure, and 2 slips from Mr. H_____'s office.

12-4   Subject made the statement that William _____ needed some material #AN402 for his apartment for drapes, bedspread and blankets, as well as to cover furniture. Consequently, several of the men took off 14 to 15 yards of material, cut it in half, wrapped it, and laid it aside. Then subject obtained 6 or 7 yards of the material for his own use. Later, subject took approximately 8 to 9 yards of material #290 and obtained help from another employee in wrapping same. Later in the evening, subject attempted to retrieve the original stolen material intended for William _____ but discovered that half of it had already been stolen and expressed the thought that it had been taken out by _____. The material that remained was taken out by subject, past the guard, and unwrapped. The guard said nothing.

12-7   At approximately 10:55 p.m. subject was observed punching out the time card of Roger _____, who had left the plant at 6:00 p.m. in an intoxicated condition.

12-9   Subject was observed at quitting time carrying out 5 to 6 yards of material #402 which had been obtained earlier off the end of a run.

12-10   Subject was observed punching out the time card of an unidentified employee at quitting time. It is believed that the other employee had left work at approximately 8:15 p.m.

12-14   At approximately 10 p.m. subject was observed in the company of Tom _____, while he obtained approximately 12 to 14 yards of a patterned Monofil material, approximately 50 inches wide, from the scrap box. Subject wrapped same in brown paper.

12-15   Subject was seen punching out the time card of Jim _____ at 11 p.m. Jim _____ had left the plant at 9 p.m. but had had an automobile accident at 9:40 p.m., which was subsequently printed in the local newspaper.

12-17   Subject obtained liquor and other items for a party on this date with $18 which was given to him by Floyd _____. After becoming intoxicated, subject was overheard to admit to another employee that he had stolen an unknown quantity of masking tape for a painter in Saratoga. Subject is believed to be responsible for breaking the lock on the door of the office in which the party was held on that night.

Manpower

One of the early problems that must be given consideration by the security director is that of manpower for the closing of the investigation. The number of security personnel assigned will depend on the number of suspects and whether or not the company has been organized by a labor union. The short-range objective should be to get through with preliminary statements from the bulk of the prime suspects by the end of the first evening. If this can be accomplished, then the security director has sufficient psychological momentum going into the second day so that union efforts to thwart the investigation should prove largely ineffective. For example, if the investigation summary indicates a total of thirty possible suspects, twenty of whom can be considered prime suspects, then the investigation team should contain at least eight or ten personnel.

Most of the members of the team should be expert interrogators, able to perform in a low-key manner in a one-on-one situation. At least one member of the team should be a qualified polygraph examiner if polygraph examinations are to be part of the closing of the case. Another member of the team should be adept at making searches for the possible recovery of contraband. A good secretary or stenographer is also indispensable. Experience has shown that when it comes time to testify in court or at a labor arbitration, the secretary or stenographer will prove to be one of the more credible witnesses that the company can put on the witness stand.

The Scene of Operations

Inasmuch as the success of the operation will depend on complete secrecy and surprise of attack, the scene of operations must not be the plant itself but rather some other location so that the investigation team will not be operating in the suspects' "back yard." By having the scene of operations away from the plant, the chances of maintaining complete secrecy throughout the first day (and thus the chances of concluding the operation successfully) are greatly enhanced.

A good quality motel within a very short driving distance from the plant has been found to be the best solution. The security director must not attempt to skimp on room costs, just as he should not hesitate to bring adequate manpower for the job. Ideally, a large suite should be designated as a waiting room for suspects, with the adjoining bedroom serving as a control center and office for the director. Each of the interrogators should be assigned a room for interrogation purposes, and one room can be set up for polygraph examinations. The motel or hotel should be one that also offers room service. It is desirable to feed the suspects at mealtime in the waiting room rather than to attempt to take them into the coffee shop. It is not necessary for the various interrogation rooms to be connecting, but they should be in close proximity to the suite.

In making reservations for such motel accommodations, the security chief must be careful to use a cover story that will preserve the integrity of his plan. An adequate story has always been that of a personnel consulting firm that intends to do extensive interviews of people over a period of two or three days. This type of a cover is logical in nature and is entirely in keeping with the type of accommodations required.

Equipment Needs

The advance planning in an operation of this type also includes a list of needed equipment. If it is anticipated that a fair amount of stolen merchandise will be recovered, then possibly two vehicles should be rented, one of which should be a station wagon to transport bulkier contraband. In some extreme cases where ordinary vehicles do not suffice, it is possible to use a company truck on a short-term basis.

Typewriters and other office supplies, including shorthand books, pencils, and erasers, will be needed for taking statements. In order to process recovered evidence, boxes, bags, labels, staplers, and tags should be provided. Kraft grocery-type bags are usually sufficient and can be adapted for use with an evidence stamp that can be affixed beforehand (see Figure 8.1). Clipboards or manila file folders should be provided in the same number as the number of anticipated suspects. If the undercover agent was successful in marking any contraband with ultraviolet crayons, then of course equipment should include an ultraviolet light to be used in scanning recovered property.

Legal and Union Review

Part of the thorough planning required for an operation of this type must include a review of any union contract as well as familiarity with the local state laws governing larceny, frauds, and/or embezzlements.

Many union contracts have unusual procedures included in sections relating to disciplinary action, grievances, and arbitrations. The security chief must be aware of any restrictions in the labor contract that might have some bearing on his investigative closing. As an example, many security heads would be inclined to suspend a particular employee after interrogation and statement-taking, pending a final disposition by company management. Some union contracts, however, do not provide for suspension, and any suspension

EVIDENCE

BAG NO._____OF_____BAGS

SUSPECT:_____

ADDRESS:_____

PHONE # (   )_____SSN_____

OWNER / VICTIM:_____

LOCATION:_____

REMARKS:_____

_____

_____

I HAVE INITIALED AND DATED EACH ARTICLE, SEALED
THIS BAG AND INITIALED THE SEAL.

_____   _____
DATE   SECURITY OFFICER

Figure 8.1   Rubber stamp to be imprinted on evidence bags.

is thus considered a direct disciplinary action. The security director should avoid, at all costs, participating in disciplinary actions. In cases of this type, the lack of a suspension clause can be circumvented by simply telling the employee to remain at home, on company time, pending final disposition of his case. To remain at home on company pay for a day or two while the investigation is being completed would not be considered a disciplinary action and would not become the subject of a grievance.

The mere interrogation or processing of a union member is not considered a disciplinary action per se and therefore union representation does not have to be offered.[9] At the point of discharge,

---

[9]For a more complete discussion of union representation, see the following chapter.

however, the action does become disciplinary in nature and the union is entitled to (and should) be made a party to the discharge, whether or not the offending employee requests representation.

Many states have a number of variations in the criminal statutes covering larceny and similar offenses. A few states even have special civil rights guarantees to offenders who ultimately are prosecuted. In the state of Minnesota, for instance, an offender must be given a copy of his signed confession at the time it is signed. This holds true even though the confession is obtained by a private or corporate security representative and without any police involvement. Several other states have gone beyond the federal requirements in this regard and have similar provisions.

Although the primary objective of the security director is to separate the hard-core thieves from the company payroll, he should not overlook the possibility of successful prosecution. In fact, if the case is built along the lines of possible prosecution, separation from the payroll becomes much easier and the case has then been prepared in the proper manner in the event of a union arbitration.

With a good understanding of the various forms of larceny and embezzlement, the security chief can proceed to build his cases during the closing with an eye toward proper prosecution. For instance, in some states theft from a warehouse is considered an automatic felony regardless of the amount involved. If he is familiar with such a law, the security director can easily word any signed statement to clearly reflect that the thefts took place from a warehouse rather than simply from a company, if this is the case. In other states, theft from a warehouse has been known to be considered the same as theft from a mercantile establishment and thus falls under the larceny statutes covering shoplifting!

If the security director is fully versed in the intricate twists and turns of the state criminal statutes and the union contract, if any, he should be able to build a strong case that will have little chance of being knocked down at a later date because of some technicality.

The Briefing

Assuming that Monday morning has been chosen for the beginning of the "bust," the security manager will undoubtedly wish to move the security crew into the community and the motel on Sunday afternoon. Inasmuch as some of the members of the crew may be outsiders, not directly employed by the security department, it is highly advisable to hold a briefing on Sunday evening so that procedures can be made clear to all security personnel and any last-minute intelligence can be added to the investigative summary.

Prime Suspects. The assembled security personnel should be briefed on the principal suspects, whom they will normally encounter in the first group of employees to be interrogated. Good tactical planning requires that the suspects with the most evidence against them should be included in the "first wave." In this way, the chances are increased of picking up additional information and additional implications of new suspects not already known.

Group Leaders. In addition to prime suspects, the "first wave" should also include any strong leader of the group, such as a shop steward, who would otherwise be likely to agitate and create problems back at the plant after it was discovered that an investigation was in process. By including the leader in the first wave, the security team has left the rest of the group without leadership and has also severed primary communication lines to any outside source of help for the thieves. The effectiveness of these tactics is exemplified in the following actual case histories.

Oakland, California.   Investigation by two company undercover agents of a general merchandise warehouse firm employing approximately 150 workers had continued for approximately six months. At the end of this time, a number of prime suspects had been identified as being involved in systematic theft.

The whole work force was dominated by the single shop steward who constantly attempted to intimidate management and who was frequently successful in his efforts. During the six-month investigation, the only piece of information developed on the shop steward was the fact that on one day he had been seen entering a restricted area of the warehouse where he had no logical reason to be and in so doing had violated company rules. Although there was no other piece of information at hand regarding this shop steward, it was decided that he would be included in the first wave to be questioned at the motel and would be interrogated by the most skilled interrogator on the security team.

The interrogator was given instructions simply to keep a conversation going with the shop steward throughout the day until quitting time. It was hoped that this would break the theft group's line of communication to the union and would enable the security personnel to get the "jump" on the case during that first day's activities.

By noon of the first day, the investigation team had identified two separate theft rings within the facility, both of which were working independently but with full knowledge of the other's activity. The shop steward who had been simply targeted for neutralization turned out to be the head of the larger of the two organized theft rings!

A second case history illustrates the same basic strategy:

Detroit Michigan.   After a number of months of undercover investigation in a drug warehouse, the investigator was able to identify the shop steward in the systematic theft of prescription and other drug items on a daily basis. This shop steward customarily performed only a minimum amount of work and spent most of his time agitating the other employees and keeping the management group in a constant uproar. Over a period of years, he had become both physically and mentally intimidating, to the point where first and second line supervision gave him a wide berth. It was the union steward's practice to leave the plant approximately fifteen minutes earlier than the normal quitting time.

A decision was made to apprehend the steward at the front of the plant when he was in possession of a small quantity of stolen drug merchandise. This apprehension took place late Monday afternoon. Within several hours, written statements had been obtained, the shop steward's home had been searched and additional drugs recovered, the subject was charged and had been incarcerated. The rest of the closing of the investigation was begun the following morning. With no leadership to back them, the members of the theft ring which was operating in the plant were easily handled and processed according to plan.

Assignments. During the briefing, the director should give the other members of the security team their primary assignments. Normally, most members of the security team will be assigned an interrogation from the first wave. In this way, all suspects in the first group will be immediately interrogated upon arrival at the motel instead of first going to a waiting room. In the eight- or ten-member team referred to earlier, primary interrogation assignments would be given to the three strongest interrogators, who are able to work very rapidly. These interrogators would be concerned with what is referred to as a "quick breakthrough"—resulting in a preliminary handwritten statement. Several other interrogators might have the primary assignment as an expansion interrogator—that is, someone who can take over the interrogation after the breakthrough and expand the case more completely in keeping with facts already developed. The polygraph examiner's primary duty, of course, ultimately will be to administer all polygraph examinations. In the meantime, he might very well serve as a break-through interrogator or an expansion interrogator. Another member of the team would be assigned the responsibility of assisting the secretary in providing food at mealtimes, making searches, recovering evidence, and processing and storing contraband.

Objective. During the briefing the security chief should be sure to stress the primary objective of the closing, which normally will be to develop sufficient evidence to justify a discharge. In certain cases, it may also be possible that the primary objective could be prosecution for one reason or another, and this of course should be stressed to the team so that the case is built accordingly.

Special Instructions. Specific instructions should be given on policy regarding phone calls and food or beverages for the suspects. Each member of the security team should be told to stress the fact that the suspects are at the motel on company time, under the same conditions as if they were on the job. They should also stress the fact that if it becomes necessary to go beyond the normal quitting time, this will be on a voluntary basis and the suspects will be paid at the rate of time-and-a-half. In this regard, it is imperative that the secretary keep a detailed log of the arrival and departure times of all suspects so that exact pay times can be computed later. The suspects must also be told that they are not there under arrest. All security personnel should readily identify themselves as security representatives for the company. It is extremely important that it be made very clear that there are no policemen present. All of this is contained in an Investigation Interview Letter (see Figure 8.2). This Interview Letter is signed ahead of time by an official of the Security Department, and at the time of the interview it is requested that it be signed

Date _____

Dear _____:

This will confirm our conversation of today, _____ 19___. You have consented to an interview with me to discuss an investigation of _____.

Please understand that the persons interviewing you are company security representatives and are not connected with local law enforcement agencies. If there are any appointments which you are unable to attend because of this interview or some other personal inconvenience has developed, telephones are available for you to make whatever calls are necessary. I have explained and you understand that this interview is being conducted on company time and you will be paid your normal rate of pay.

If this interview continues beyond your normal working hours, you will be paid accordingly. You are free to stop this interview and leave at any time.

Please indicate your understanding of these arrangements by signing below. We thank you in advance for your help and cooperation in this investigation.

Sincerely,

By _____

_____

_____

Figure 8.2 Investigation interview letter.

by the suspect and one copy given to him and the other copy retained by the Security Department. In the event that a suspect refuses to sign the Investigation Interview Letter, it should simply be read to him in the presence of another witness and then signed by both witnesses to certify the fact that it had been read to the suspect.

Monitoring the Waiting Room. The team should also be made aware of the conditions that will prevail in the waiting room as the day wears on. The waiting room should be monitored constantly by some member of the security staff not otherwise occupied at the time. The reason for the monitoring is not so much to act as a guard but simply to psychologically deter the suspects from discussing the case.

Protecting Investigative Data. Admonitions should also be given to the interrogators on the security of their investigative summaries and clipboards that contain the individual statements and related papers for each suspect. They should be told that under no circumstances are they ever to leave an interrogation room containing a suspect and not carry along the aforementioned articles.

Firearms. If certain members of the security team are to be armed, then the proper admonition must be given concerning the display of any firearms. Under no circumstances should a firearm worn by a security person be visible to an employee suspect. If firearms are necessary for the recovery of merchandise, then jackets must be worn and kept buttoned at all times. Of course, firearms should never be carried in violation of any state or local laws.

Director's Authority. During the briefings, the investigation director must make it clear that he and he alone will be the boss of the operation. Accordingly, all press and police relations must be handled by the director and no one else.

"Pep Talk." The briefing can end with a psychological preparation of the investigation team: a "pep talk" pointing to the anticipated success of the operation and also emphasizing that it will be a team effort and no "grandstanding" by individual interrogators will be appreciated.

The Control Sheet

The interrogators and other security team members should also be instructed on how to report their progress throughout the day and how to receive new assignments as the day progresses. This is normally done through the use of a control sheet maintained by the director of the operation. Experience has shown that in processing large numbers of suspects over a period of days, it is easy to lose track of particular suspects and their various stages of processing at any given time. A control sheet is necessary to maintain proper records. The control sheet contains various columns headed as follows:

NAME

AGE

JOB

YEARS SERVICE

STATEMENTS:
  PRELIMINARY
  EXPANSION
  FORMAL

SELLING

POLYGRAPH

RECOVERIES:
  MERCHANDISE
  CASH

COMPANY ACTION:
  PRELIMINARY
  FINAL

POLICE ACTION

REMARKS

In addition to maintaining control of the investigation and the orderly processing of suspects, the security director ultimately will have to be able to provide top management with detailed information on the degree of involvement of each particular suspect. Furthermore, in legal action that may follow, such as an arbitration, it may be necessary to reveal to a labor arbitrator the complete scope of the investigation and the degree of culpability from one suspect to another. This is especially true if management ultimately decides to draw a line in an attempt to rehabilitate minor offenders as opposed to major offenders.

Stakeouts

In the advance planning for a closing operation, the security director may wish to provide the capability for stakeouts of certain key suspects' homes during the first evening of the closing. This holds true especially in cases involving large numbers of suspects where it was not possible to initially process each of the prime suspects on the first day. It must be presumed that many of the employees who have not yet been interrogated will learn of the investigation during the evening of the first day. As a result, experience has shown that where large quantities of stolen merchandise are involved, the contraband may very well be moved from one location to another. By use of a stakeout on key suspects' homes, this diversionary tactic can often be surveilled if not, in fact, intercepted.

Police Assistance

Prior to the advent of the *Miranda* decision (see Chapter 9), police assistance and participation were not only helpful but in some cases highly desirable. Since the *Miranda* decision by the United States Supreme Court, private security persons are required to operate under the same ground rules as the police department if the police are brought into the case and actively participate with the company security personnel. For this reason, the security director should be hesitant about making any type of a formal crime report. Under most circumstances, the police should not be involved in the case, as to do so would only hamper the efforts of the company's security personnel and greatly complicate the whole procedure. If any police assistance is needed, it should be unofficial in nature and only advisory in form. Active participation by the police, if any, should come at the conclusion of the case and then only in those cases where there is a clear-cut desire to initiate prosecution.

Bringing in the First Group of Suspects

Because the success of the closing operation depends upon maintaining secrecy throughout the first day, the method of getting the suspects to the motel is critical. The most desirable way is for a trusted member of first line supervision to round up the first four or five prime suspects and simply ask them to accompany him in his automobile to a meeting with a higher-ranking executive. The supervisor should not be aware himself that an investigation is about to commence; he should simply be given instructions over the telephone by the higher-ranking executive and told whom he should bring to the meeting. The supervisor can then be briefed at the motel by the security director for the role he should play with succeeding waves of suspects. Another pretext that has been used successfully is a request for the suspects to accompany the supervisor to a particular motel to aid in setting up merchandising displays.

In some rare cases, complicated by militant union members, it may not be possible for a supervisor to attempt to bring out the suspects himself. This is especially true where there is reason to believe that one or more of the suspects might be armed, in possession of drugs, or otherwise so "street-wise" as to see through the pretext. In this case, it is much simpler to have the supervisor or personnel department summon a particular suspect (only one at a time) to the front of the plant, where several security representatives can identify themselves and request the suspect to accompany them. Experience has shown that where this is done properly and with great skill, refusal on the part of the suspect is unlikely. In the rare event of a refusal, however, the security personnel should be instructed to immediately take the suspect into a private, secluded office and start the interrogation at the plant. This procedure is not desirable but would have to be a final fall-back position in the unlikely event of a refusal.

If the first wave of suspects are brought out by a supervisor, the same precision planning and speed must be employed by security personnel at the motel that are required in a pickup at the plant door. Normally, each of the security personnel will be assigned an individual suspect by name. As the car approaches the predesignated spot at one of the motel rooms, each member of the security team calls out the name of his suspect as the group alights from the vehicle. With each person's name being so enunciated, there is no time for discussion between the suspects. In a matter of ten seconds or less, if the operation is handled properly, each suspect should be ensconced in one of the interrogation rooms with his assigned interrogator.

The first order of business on the part of the interrogator is to secure a signature on the Investigation Interview Letter. The interrogator also should have positioned the chairs in the room in advance so that the suspect is between the interrogator and the door. The interrogator should never place himself between the suspect and the door so that charges of false imprisonment can be largely avoided.

Succeeding Groups of Suspects

Succeeding waves will probably not be as large in number, since there will not be sufficient security personnel on hand to start an immediate interrogation. However, as the day goes on and the situation becomes less critical, the third and fourth waves can often be simply deposited in the waiting room upon their arrival at the motel. By this time, certain suspects from the first and second groups who have already confessed will be in the waiting room. Recovered stolen merchandise may also be present and in the process of being inventoried. This whole atmosphere then works psychologically in favor of the security personnel, and a group psychology seems to take hold. Subsequent confessions are much easier to obtain than those earlier in the day. To confess at this point seems the natural thing to do, as everybody else has been doing the same thing, and a spirit of "cooperation" seems to prevail among those in the waiting room. To the new arrivals, the sight of stolen merchandise being processed is especially devastating and proves to be a powerful mental conditioner for what follows in the interrogation room.

CHAPTER 9

INTERROGATIONS, CONFESSIONS, AND EVIDENCE RECOVERIES

Protecting the Undercover Agent

If there is even the remotest possibility of a labor arbitration or a criminal prosecution arising from an internal theft investigation, the security chief should build his case with the view of ultimately winning in that type of legal setting. One of the most effective tools for the company in a labor arbitration, or even a prosecution, is the testimony of an undercover agent. All of the legal arguments regarding interrogation atmosphere, voluntariness of confession, consent to search, etc., pale alongside the testimony of any undercover agent who can state, with eyewitness certainty, that a particular defendant did steal company property.

If the agent can be used as a surprise witness, or as a rebuttal witness in a criminal prosecution, the effect of his testimony is overpowering and almost insures a guilty finding. On the other hand, if union lawyers or defense attorneys learn of the existence of an undercover agent, their whole strategy will be based on utilizing the concept of entrapment as a defense. The successful use of entrapment as a defense requires some preparation on the part of the defense attorney, in consultation with the defendant. If the undercover operative is a surprise witness, this necessary preparation time is usually not available, and the defense of entrapment is only a makeshift one at best.

Keeping all this in mind, the security director must make every effort to impress upon his investigation crew that the existence of an undercover agent is to be concealed at all costs. In writing the investigation summary, any reference to the undercover agent should be made as "another employee." Under no circumstances should interrogators ever use the work of the undercover agent to facilitate obtaining a confession. It is much better to spend a few extra hours' effort in interrogation, or wait for implications from fellow thieves, than to expose the undercover operative.

On rare occasions, it may be necessary to partially expose the undercover agent in an effort to break down the resistance of an offender and obtain a confession. If this does become absolutely necessary and is used only as a last resort, then the agent should be placed in the role of another offending employee who, under great interrogation pressure, has implicated himself and one or more of his fellow workers. In such a case a confrontation should be arranged between the undercover agent and a non-cooperating offender. Otherwise, the undercover agent should be processed routinely along with the other thieves, so that they all gain the impression that he, too, has been caught and will ultimately lose his job.

In the trauma of a "bust," the fact that one employee implicates another, even though it is used during a confrontation, is finally regarded as "just one of those things." The confronting employee may ultimately be considered weak of character, and a particular thief may continue to hold a grudge, but at least criminal defense strategy or union legal tactics will not be altered by one employee confronting another and thus obtaining a confession. In contrast, if an offender is confronted by an undercover agent, the confession may be easily obtained, but at that point the groundwork for the defense of entrapment has been laid.

Discretion in Processing Female Suspects

The processing of female suspects in a motel setting during a "bust" dictates prudence on the part of the director. In the author's thirty-three years of experience in large-scale internal theft cases, most of them including women suspects, never has a female made a charge of improper conduct towards any member of the interrogation team. Even though the interrogation is a one-on-one situation often conducted by a male interrogator with a female suspect in a motel room, the following precautions will usually suffice to discourage frivolous charges of improper conduct.

Chairs, as stated earlier, should be positioned in such a way that the female suspect is between the interrogator and the door. Male interrogators should be instructed that, when they take a female suspect into the interrogation room, the door should be left open three to six inches at all times. Within several minutes of the commencement of the interrogation, a female secretary should enter the room and ask the female suspect if she would care for coffee or a soft drink. This action immediately makes clear to the female suspect that there is another female in attendance in the general area. If the suspect wants something to drink, the female secretary will enter the interrogation room again within the next five or ten minutes with the desired refreshment. On the other hand, if the suspect declines the offer, then the secretary can re-enter the room in about fifteen or twenty minutes and renew the offer of refreshment. Thus, she has entered the room easily on at least two occasions, and it becomes fixed in the suspect's mind that persons may enter or leave the room at will, and that any loud shouting or screaming would be immediately overheard in the outside corridor.

Female suspects in the waiting room present no problem whatsoever, as there are usually other suspects present and a female secretary is in attendance.

During the administration of a polygraph test, it is not possible for the motel door to be left ajar, or for anyone to enter and leave at will. There are other factors, however, that tend to mitigate this potential problem. The female suspect at this point has spent several periods of time with different interrogators in the various rooms in a one-on-one situation, and generally realizes there will be no opportunity for a charge of misconduct. She is likely to expect the same situation in the polygraph examination room as in the interrogation rooms.

The male polygraph examiner himself is used to handling female examinees in the course of his regular business. Mentally, he is quite used to being alone with females in confined quarters. Through his training and years of experience on the job, he has learned to conduct himself with such a professional air that the female immediately recognizes his demeanor and attitude as being similar to what she might expect during an examination by her family physician. The fact that a polygraph examiner must come into physical contact with the female when attaching the instrument to her body is largely neutralized by the polygraphist's approach towards the subject. This is an approach that must be entirely different from that used by the initial interrogators who were attempting to obtain a confession. Here, the polygraph examiner is working with the female suspect in an effort to verify the truthfulness of her statements.

The *Miranda* Decision

In *Miranda v Arizona*, a landmark decision in 1966, the United States Supreme Court ruled that when a suspect is taken into police custody, or from the moment that an interviewee becomes a police suspect, that person must be advised of his constitutional rights. In essence, these rights consist of the advice that any statement made by the suspect can be used against him in criminal court; that he is not required to make any type of statement; that the interrogation must be halted if the suspect so requests; that the suspect may request the presence of an attorney during the proceedings; and that if he is unable to afford his own legal counsel, one will be provided.

The result of the *Miranda* decision was to revolutionize the criminal justice system and, in effect, to reduce the number of police interrogations and subsequent confessions in the processing of criminal suspects. The decision was meant to govern the activities of sworn police officers and did not include private or corporate security personnel. In other words, *Miranda* is inapplicable to non-custodial questioning by private citizens.[10] This exclusion has been in effect since the original *Miranda* decision, and at least up to the date of publication of this text. Some authorities speculate, however, that eventually the rule may be extended to trained security personnel even though they are not sworn police officers. It must be pointed out that in the ten years since the original draft of this text, the *Miranda* rule has not been extended to trained security personnel.

An exception to the above guidelines is the case where a security agent is also a sworn police officer. A number of security agents have been given auxiliary or special police commissions in order to facilitate their work. The existence of such a commission means that the security agent is obliged to give the *Miranda* warning prior to any interrogation effort. For this reason, many corporate security departments abolished the practice of their agents being special or auxiliary police officers after the *Miranda* decision.

The only other exception to the exclusion is in the event that the private security agents seek and obtain the active assistance of local police officials in the handling of the case. If the local police participate in the case, then their ground rules must be observed by private security personnel. This includes observance of the *Miranda* warning and any other rules of criminal procedure that police follow. This is a powerful argument against inviting the police to participate in a private company's investigative efforts. In effect, it points up the superior freedom enjoyed by security personnel in handling their own cases, compared to the police in handling criminal suspects.

Union Representation

In a 6–3 decision, the United States Supreme Court has ruled that employees who belong to unions are entitled to union representation during questioning by an employer or the employer's agent.

In two separate but similar cases, *N.L.R.B.* v *J. Weingarten, Inc.*[11] and *I.L.G.W.U.* v *Quality Manufacturing Company et al.*,[12] the high

---

[10]*Yates* v *United States* 384 F. 2d 586 (5th Cir. 1967).
[11]*N.L.R.B.* v *J. Weingarten, Inc.* 485 F. 2d 1135 (1973).
[12]*I.L.G.W.U.* v *Quality Manufacturing Co.* 95 S. Ct. 972 (1975).

court ruled that such interrogation that can result in disciplinary action entitles the employee to representation if he requests same. Failure to honor such a request "interferes with, restrains and coerces the individual right of the employee to engage in concerted activities for mutual aid or protection."

Without question, the decision is bound to complicate the work of many security officials whose companies are organized by a union. The court did *not* state that representation must be offered in all cases—only if it is desired. Furthermore, the court *did* state that the employer or his agent may elect to terminate the interview if such a request for union representation is made. This option can be pointed out to the employee, as well as the fact that the employee would not gain any of the benefits that might result from such an interview. In other words, the employer may proceed on a course of action with whatever facts are already at hand, and the employee may take his chances with the consequences.

If the interview or questioning proceeds with a shop steward or business agent present, the court affirms the union's role as follows:

> The representative is present to assist the employee, and may attempt to clarify the facts or suggest other employees who may have knowledge of them. The employer, however, is free to insist that he is only interested, at that time, in hearing the employee's own account of the matter under investigation.[13]

It is well established in labor law that an employee has a duty and obligation to cooperate with his employer during an investigation. By the same token, many lawyers feel that a deliberate attempt by a union representative to block or interfere with an investigation constitutes an unfair labor practice on the part of the union.

In a footnote to its decision, the court also makes reference to polygraph tests and the need for union representation. The court is not specific on this issue, but some legal authorities feel that the question of union representation could be satisfied by allowing the representative to be present during a general discussion of the polygraph test and a review of the relevant questions. He should not be allowed to sit in on the examination itself.

The court's decision on union representation has changed procedures very little in the intervening years. Generally speaking, most employees are not aware of the court's decision and therefore do not ask for union representation during a major "bust," especially where the elements of surprise and adequate manpower are viable factors. Once the word spreads among employee groups, however, the result of the court's decision will virtually dictate that security directors

---

[13]*Ibid.*

must develop sufficient evidence beforehand that would enable the case to stand on its own merits in the absence of a confession. Moreover, if such strong evidence is developed beforehand, the interrogator's chances of dissuading the employee from his initial request of demanding union representation will be greater. If an employee feels that the company has a solid case against him, and that if he persists in his request for union representation the interview will be discontinued by the employer, resulting in the employee's subsequent discharge, he will be more inclined to wish to discuss the matter privately. He may even hold out some hope in his mind that the employer may allow him a chance for rehabilitation and probation.

An informal survey taken of some key security directors of major corporations indicates that most plan to develop strong investigations and will not attempt any interviews in the presence of the shop steward or business agent of the local union.

As in any far-reaching court decision, there are always additional rulings and decisions growing out of the original. Three of the more notable decisions that have further clarified the *Weingarten* rule are presented below.

Lennox Industries Case. . .Further interpretation of "The Weingarten Rule"— Lennox Industries Inc. v N.L.R.B. CA 5 NOR 79-3890, 79-3894, 2-17-81.   Foreman Ary approaches worker Paul Nestle—deliberate slowdown. Nestle asks for shop steward—refused because as Lennox later said—no disciplinary action ever intended. Fifth Circuit court says— clear violation of Weingarten. 8th & 9th Circuits say representation is required only when discipline is "probable" or "seriously considered." 5th Circuit disagrees with this and says that above is inconsistent with Supreme Court's original decision.

Southwestern Bell v N.L.R.B. #80-2072 (BNA 10-17-82 #32).   On December 7, 1977, Billy Hubbard, a security officer for Bell, received information that a pair of climbing hooks and a safety belt bearing the Bell System markings were on display at a pawn shop. Because Bell does not sell its equipment, Hubbard suspected that the items had been stolen and pawned and, on December 9, accompanied by a Houston police officer, he went to the shop and obtained the name, address, driver's license, and physical description of the person who had pawned the equipment in question. Charles Gottschalk was the name provided by the shopkeeper. Hubbard confirmed that Charles Gottschalk in Bell's employ lived at the same address, had the same driver's license number and fit the physical description provided by the owner of the pawnshop. Based on this information, a meeting was set with Gottschalk for December 14 to allow him an opportunity to give his side of the story.

Gottschalk consulted with McQuiller (the Union Steward) prior to the meeting and was advised not to say anything.

Hubbard requested that McQuiller not answer any of the questions put to Gottschalk.

The board decided that Bell violated Gottschalk's right to union representation at the December 14, 1977, investigatory interview by requesting the representative not to interfere with questioning. This decision was set aside finding no such violation.

The employer has no duty to bargain with the union representative at an investigatory interview. "This representative is present to assist the employee and may attempt to clarify the facts or suggest other employees who may have knowledge of them."

The security officer, Mr. Hubbard, made the following request of Mr. McQuiller, according to Mr. Hubbard's testimony on direct examination at the hearing. "I told Mr. McQuiller that I don't want him to answer the questions, but I wanted Mr. Gottschalk to answer the questions, and then after we were through if he had any questions, then he could ask them, but I wanted Mr. Gottschalk to be the one that answers the questions."

Mark McQuiller testified on direct examination at the hearing that Mr. Hubbard's request took the following form: "At that time, he told me not to say anything or answer any questions that he would pose direct." Tommy Hataway, the General Counsel's other witness to the incident, testified at the hearing to the following: "Then, before he went any further, he looked directly at Mark and said, "I'm going to ask Charles some questions. I don't want you to say anything, I want him to answer in his own words."

In the decision in the present case, the board has, therefore, made an unwarranted extension of the employee's *Weingarten* rights. It is clear that investigatory confrontation without restricted union representation is an unfair labor practice. *Lennox Industries v. NLRB*, 637 F. 2d 340 (5th Cir. 1981) and an employer cannot discipline an employee for refusing in an investigatory interview to answer questions without union assistance. The union representative has the right to make additions and clarifications to the meeting. This right is not without restrictions, however. The limitations in the instant case were within the perimeters set forth by the Supreme Court in *Weingarten* and did not interfere with McQuiller's ability to assist Gottschalk, to clarify facts, or to bring additional relevant facts to Hubbard's attention. We therefore hold that Gottschalk's *Weingarten* rights were not violated.

Montgomery Ward v N.L.R.B. No. 81-1248 (BNA 12-17-81 #242).   Two workers who admitted stealing merchandise from their employer are not entitled to reinstatement merely because the company refused their requests for union representation at an investigative interview, the U.S. Court of Appeals for the eighth circuit rules. The Court overturns an N.L.R.B. order requiring Montgomery Ward & Co., Inc., to provide reinstatement and back pay.

Although there is "substantial evidence" to support a determination that the employer violated section 8(a)(1) of the Taft-Hartley Act by denying union representation as required under the U.S. Supreme Court holding in *N.L.R.B.* v. *Weingarten, Inc.* 88 LRRM 2689, the Courts find that the board lacks authority to order the reinstatement of employees discharged for good cause.

During the course of a security investigation, Wards discovered that the two employees had been stealing merchandise from their respective departments. When the security investigator attempted to arrange an interview regarding the thefts, each employee requested union representation. The two were told that the security interviews would not be conducted if a union representative were called and that the entire matter instead would be turned over to management and the police.

The two employees then both signed an interview consent form, proceeded with the interview, and signed a statement admitting that they had stolen merchandise from the company. Both of them offered to make restitution. After reviewing the results of the investigation, Wards fired both workers.

Finding that the failure to permit requested union assistance at the interviews constituted a violation, a board ALJ (administrative law judge) recommended reinstatement and back pay for one of the employees, who had recanted his confession. The board agreed and added that the firm should expunge any record of discharge from that employee's files and should provide back pay for the other worker.

Judges Bright, Ross, and Larsen find clear evidence that the firings were a direct result of the admitted thefts and not the result of the employees' insistence on the presence of a union steward. Despite the violation by the employer, the court finds that reinstatement and back pay is "clearly prohibited" by the language of the act.

The same issue was resolved by the Appeals Courts, the Per Curiam opinion says, in *N.L.R.B.* v. *Potter Electrical Signal Co.,* 101 LRRM 2378, when it found that section 10 (c) of the Act precludes an order of back pay and reinstatement when it is clear that employees were discharged for good cause and not for requesting union assistance at an investigatory interview.

"In this case, like *Potter,* the employees effected their own discharge by stealing and the section 8(a)(1) violation was simply incidental to the investigation which preceded the firing," the Court concludes. It denies enforcement of N.L.R.B. determinations concerning back pay and reinstatement.

Voluntariness and Other Considerations

Without having to contend with the *Miranda* decision, the main issue for the security director to be concerned with on written statements is their voluntariness. In the legal proceedings following the "bust," some defendants will attempt to repudiate their confession with arguments such as: "I was scared and I didn't realize what I was signing"; "I was told if I signed the paper I would not lose my job"; "I was told that the statements would only be used for the insurance company and that nothing would happen to me"; "I was told I would be turned over to the police if I did not cooperate"; "I was kept in a motel room and was not allowed to leave."

The above are just a few of the many and varied stratagems employed by defendants in labor arbitrations or criminal prosecutions in an effort to refute their previously made statements. Knowing all this, the security director must incorporate into all the statements certain features that will tend to counter many of the above arguments and make it more difficult for a defendant or his attorney to successfully attack the validity of the confessions. The atmosphere throughout each day of the investigation should be one of informality and friendliness, and should uphold human dignity.

For many years the techniques outlined in Chapters 7 and 8 of this text have met the test in lower courts and labor arbitrations successfully. Finally, in *U.S. v Maddox* (1974),[14] the United States Court of Appeals for the Fifth Circuit upheld many of these techniques. The United States Supreme Court declined to accept a further review of this case on a writ of *certiorari*, thus establishing that legal history had been made concerning many of the techniques advocated by this text. In illustration, we quote from the court's own language of this case:

> The voluntariness of K's confession is challenged on appeal. The private investigators arranged for employee suspects to be questioned at a local motel, concerning the missing merchandise. The employees, still on the company payroll and not under arrest, were maintained at company expense in a casual atmosphere. A TV room, sandwiches, and snacks were provided. The employees received their normal pay, including overtime during the questioning. Their freedom to leave was equivalent to that while "on the job." It was in this context that K confessed his activities.[15]

---

[14]Vol. 492 F 2d. 73 2611 (1974).
[15]Ibid.

Outside Suspects

In many cases persons who are not directly employed by the company may be involved in internal theft rings, and it becomes necessary to consider a method of prosecuting such outsiders. Realizing that he does not have the same degree of psychological control over an outsider as over an employee, the security director knows that an outsider's presence at the motel for processing must be completely voluntary. Experience has shown that many outside suspects will cooperate if approached during the first day of the "bust" by several agents who identify themselves as security representatives of the company. The majority of these people usually are willing to accompany the agents back to the motel for questioning. In trying to analyze their motives for compliance, one can only assume that, knowing they are deeply involved in the theft, they reach the conclusion that they would much rather take their chances with company personnel than with the police. Of course, security agents must be careful not to use the threat of police involvement as a means of gaining their cooperation.

Once at the motel, the outside suspect must again be made aware of the fact that he is not under arrest and is free to leave if he so chooses. Other than that, he should be processed like any other company employee, but the processing should be expedited because of the fact that he is there on his own time. Following completion of his processing, the outside suspect should be returned to his home or place of business. If he is to be prosecuted, his individual case should be included with all the others that ultimately are turned over to the police or district attorney following completion of the case.

Occasionally, it will be determined that an outsider is the employee of another company. In that case, it may even be possible to gain the cooperation of the other company's security department in providing for interrogation facilities on the other company's premises.

The Preliminary Statement

As discussed in Chapter 8, the initial interrogation of the suspect is designed to obtain a quick breakthrough. This means that the primary objective is to obtain a written statement of any significant theft initially admitted to by the suspect. Experience has shown that if a case is properly prepared beforehand, and sufficient information has been developed, as contained in the investigation summary, a preliminary statement can be obtained from most suspects within the first fifteen to thirty minutes of interrogation time. The main objective here should be a statement that will sustain a discharge, if challenged in a labor arbitration. If at all possible, the statement should be in the suspect's own handwriting, and should contain sufficient information to hold up under attack on *voir dire*. An example of such a preliminary statement, which has been upheld throughout the years in various legal proceedings, is shown in Figure 9.1.

Baltimore, Md.
Jan. 9, 19

My name is John Smith. I am 40 years old and live at 1234 Main Street, Baltimore. I am employed as a shipping assistant at Acme Products 567 South Street, and have worked for the company for 1½ years.

During the last 6 months of my employment, I have taken without permission or payment property and merchandise belonging to Acme as follows: 7 full rolls of piece goods, 2 partial rolls of piece goods, one hand truck, and about 6 shirts. I took the shirts out at lunch time by hiding them under my clothes. My friend Bill Jones who is a truck driver helped me get the piece goods out.

This statement is true and voluntary. No promises or threats have been made to me. I knew this was wrong but ask the company to give me another chance to prove myself.

WITNESSED:

John Smith
1234 Main St.
Baltimore, Md.
10 AM

Figure 9.1   Preliminary statement.

The Expansion Statement

Following the preliminary statement and a brief pause for refreshments in the waiting room, a second interrogator will normally take the suspect to another interrogation room in an effort to expand the information already obtained. This will be recorded in a so-called addendum statement. Many times, the approach used by the initial interrogator for a quick breakthrough will almost dictate the necessity for a new interrogation face—one who can utilize an entirely different approach necessary to expanding the degree of involvement.

The purpose of the expansion statement is to develop knowledge of coworkers' involvement, collusion, methods of operation (M.O.), location, etc. The expansion interrogator may very well become more aggressive in his interrogation than did the breakthrough interrogator. There is less chance of losing the subject during expansion than during the initial interrogation.

In any addendum statement, the time and date should be noted and reference made to the earlier statement made in the initial interrogation. Here again, the statement should be in the subject's own handwriting if at all possible. It is convenient to use an NCR-type triplicate paper for the preliminary and any addendum statements. This type of paper lends itself easily to handwritten statements and produces its own copies, thus eliminating the necessity for carbon paper. All that is required is a firm writing surface and the use of a ballpoint pen. An example of an expansion or addendum statement is shown in Figure 9.2.

The Narrative Statement

Although the narrative statement is very popular with insurance investigators and with certain law enforcement agencies, its use is advocated by the author primarily under two circumstances. In a major investigation, where a preliminary statement has been obtained, and this in turn has been followed by one or more addendum statements, it may be desirable to finish the processing of an individual by taking the narrative statement and attempting to incorporate into it all the various points developed, rather than having them appear in different statements. In other words, the narrative statement can be considered a summary of a suspect's involvement in the case. This approach should primarily be used where the director feels that no prosecution, or any other type of legal activity, criminal or civil, is contemplated. Also, the narrative statement is generally not recommended for use in building a bonding claim.

Jan 9, 19
11:45AM

My name is John Smith. I wish to add to the statement which I made earlier today. After discussing the thefts with Mr. Harris, I realize I did not tell everything in the first statement.

Altogether Bill Jones and I have been stealing rolls of piece goods for almost one year. On Wednesdays I am left in charge of the shipping and receiving doors during lunch time. Bill usually gets there with his truck about 12:45 and we usually put something on. Bill gives me half of what he gets for the cloth. I guess I have received about $1,000.— for my share. Bill says he sells the cloth to his cousin who lives in Pennsylvania. We have taken somewhere between 30 and 40 full or partial rolls.

I make this second statement so that the truth will be out. I want to cooperate and I know I will probably loose my job. I am being well treated.

John Smith

WITNESSED:

Figure 9.2 Expansion statement.

A further use of the narrative statement is at times when management must act in a situation where an employee has been apprehended and no professional security personnel are quickly available to take a statement. Here, it is to the advantage of management to get as many of the facts as possible into one statement.

The main objection to a narrative statement is the fact that it is more self-serving than other types of statements. Unlike the preliminary statement, where only the first and last paragraphs are conceded to be dictated, the narrative statement is usually dictated in its entirety, and it is the interrogator's attempt to tell the suspect's story for him. In such an attempt, the language used in the statement is almost never exactly the type that might actually be used by the suspect. The statement itself, of course, tells a neat, concise story, which clearly benefits the investigator rather than the subject. At no point in the narrative statement does the subject clearly have an opportunity to say anything he may wish to include in such a statement. A sample narrative statement is reproduced in Figure 9.3.

```
                          SPECIMEN OF
                       NARRATIVE STATEMENT

                                                     August 1, 19


"I, John Doe, age 23, am employed by _____ Company, Newark, New Jersey,
as a shipping sorter.  I have worked for _____ Company since June,
1962.

Today, at about 1:30 PM, I took an empty box and went to the _____
section, where I removed the following items from section 8 (list):

_____

_____

_____


I fully realized that this was the property of my employer and I realized that I
was stealing because I intended not to pay for them but to sell them to my cousin
who lives near me.  I carried the box down to the shipping room where I hid it
until the end of the day.  No one in authority gave me permission to bring the
box down, as I came down the back stairs when no one was looking.

After quitting at 5:00 PM, I went to the rear of the building and entered the
shipping room where I picked up the box.  Mr. Williams, the Foreman, caught me
just as I jumped down off the rear dock.

I knew I was doing wrong and stealing, and now want to do right by the company
by telling the truth.  I put my initials on all the merchandise I stole, and it
has been sealed up by Mr. Williams, in my presence, for safekeeping.  I also
wrote about the items on the outside of the bag and signed my name.

I have made this statement of my own free will and voluntarily.  No promises or
threats were made to me, and I feel that I have been treated fairly.  I made
this statement so that the truth would be known."

                                      Signed:



                                      John Doe
                                      Newark, New Jersey

Witnessed:

Mr. J. B. Williams, Foreman
Miss Jean Smith, Secretary
```

Figure 9.3 Sample narrative statement.

The Formal Statement

Although more time-consuming and involved, the formal statement is by far the strongest type of statement an investigator can obtain. It is a statement that by its very nature forces the suspect to utilize his own language and his own descriptions of events that have taken place. By virtue of the fact that it is first taken down in shorthand by a stenographer, it insures the presence of another witness throughout the actual taking of the statement. If structured properly, the statement can overcome not only any questions of voluntariness, but also can give sufficient detail upon which to base specific criminal charges of larceny. This type of statement has withstood the challenge of time in many court jurisdictions throughout the United States. To put it simply, if the statement is properly taken, there is no way the suspect can repudiate it at a later date.

Figure 9.4 is a sample prototype for a formal statement designed to cover larceny cases. In embezzlement cases, or any other case involving various forms of documentation, the only difference is that each piece of documentation should be read into the statement. That is, where certain records have been altered or forged, each individual record should be presented to the suspect and identified in the statement, and the suspect should be asked to examine the document and initial it. This is then acknowledged in the statement as one of the documents utilized in the crime.

In the event of a case involving collusion of two or more suspects, it is sometimes desirable to have the second suspect present in the room when the statement is being taken, and to indicate in the heading of the statement that the additional suspect is present. Furthermore, it is often desirable to have the second suspect sign as a witness on the statement of the first suspect, if possible. This whole situation is then reversed when taking the second suspect's formal statement. The fact that various members of a theft ring or collusive theft are present and witnessing each other's statements is a powerful binder on the whole case.

Searches, Seizures, and Recoveries

While a preliminary or addendum statement is being taken, a suspect will often indicate that he has placed stolen property in his home or in some other area. If he has not volunteered this information, then it should be explored by the interrogator and an attempt made to determine the existence of such stolen contraband that can be recovered. At this point, after he has made one or more handwritten statements of guilt, there seems to be little problem in obtaining the

S T A T E M E N T

Statement made by William G. Doe, employee of_____
Company, in the office of Richard Long, Plant Manager, at 123 Washington Road,
Baltimore, Maryland. This statement was taken at 3.00 PM, January 5, 19 ,
in the presence of Richard Long, Plant Manager, and Mary White, stenographer.
Questions, unless otherwise indicated, are by Thomas Jones, Security Officer
for the Company.

Q. What is your name and address?

A.

Q. What is your age, date of birth, place of birth?

A.

Q. Where are you employed, in what capacity, and for how long?

A.

Q. Can you tell us the name of the grammar school you attended?

A.

Q. What was your mother's maiden name?

A.

Q. Before proceeding further, do you realize that you do not have to make
    this statement - it could be used against you?

A.

Q. Why do you wish to make this statement?

A.

Q. Do you realize that you can refuse to answer any of the questions in this
    statement?

A.

Q. In connection with your business as a_____
    for_____Company, do you have occasion to
    handle items of merchandise which are the property of your employer?

A.

Q. In connection with your handling this merchandise, have you ever stolen
    and removed any of it from the_____?

A.

Q. When you took this merchandise, did anyone in authority give you
    permission to take it?

A.

Q. In not having permission to take the merchandise, nor paying for it,
    did you realize you were stealing and in effect committing a larceny?

A.

Figure 9.4   Sample formal statement for larceny cases.

Q. Bill, can you tell us to the best of your memory, when you first stole and removed merchandise from the_____?

A.

Q. Can you tell us the most recent occasion when you have stolen merchandise from_____? (Get details of date, time, method of removal, etc.)

A.

Q. What is the least expensive item you have stolen from_____?

A.

Q. What is the most expensive item you have stolen from_____? (Get as many details as possible).

A.

Q. What is the most merchandise you have ever stolen and removed from the _____ at any one time?

A.

MR. LONG NOW QUESTIONING:

Q. Can you remember on what day or in what month this occurred?

A.

Q. Bill, can you tell us to the best of your memory, the total amount of merchandise that you have stolen from_____?

A.

Q. On what basis do you arrive at the above figure? (Subject's answer should be at rate of so much per day, week, month or year).

A.

Q. Can you give us examples of merchandise which you have stolen which are included in these figures?

A.

Q. Can you tell us why you stole these items? For what purpose did you intend to use them? (If the items were for resale, the interrogator should get the name and address of the receiver, what items were delivered, where the items were dropped off, how much money was received, dates of deliveries, method of ordering, etc.).

A.

MR. JONES AGAIN QUESTIONING:

Q. Bill, in stealing these items, how did you manage to get them out of the_____?

A.

Figure 9.4   Continued.

Q. Since you have worked here, have you ever helped or participated in stealing with other employees?

A.

Q. Can you tell us who these employees are and just how you were involved with each one? (Here again, the interrogator should get as many details as possible - that is, who, what, when, where, why, how, etc.).

A.

Q. With regard to all of the merchandise now in your home, car, garage, etc., would you be willing to turn it over to us personally?

A.

Q. Bill, have you made this statement voluntarily and of your own free will?

A.

Q. Have any promises of reward or immunity been made to you?

A.

Q. Has anyone forced or threatened you to make this statement?

A.

Q. Can you tell us if you feel you have been abused or if you have been treated fairly?

A.

Q. Is there anything else you wish to tell us that has to do with this matter? (Interrogator should repeat this question until a "No" answer if forthcoming).

A.

Q. If, after reading this statement, and making any necessary corrections, additions, or deletions, will you be willing to sign it?

A.

"I have read this statement, and understand its content fully. The statement contains_____pages, and I have written my initials on each page in addition to signing my name on this page."

Date:_____   Signature:_____

Witnessed: Address in full:

_____   _____

_____   _____

_____

Figure 9.4   Continued.

subject's consent to a voluntary search of his home or some other area. For this purpose, experience has shown that a Consent to Search form, as shown in Figure 9.5, has proved more than adequate.

In the example shown, note that there is a portion on the bottom of the form for an additional consent to be given by the spouse. In some cases, the investigator may run into a refusal to cooperate on

---

CONSENT TO SEARCH

I, _____, age _____, admit that merchandise

stolen from _____ is presently stored at _____

_____ .
(Description and Location)

I hereby consent to take _____
(Names of persons making search)

_____

to _____, and agree to return all of such stolen
(Description and Location)

merchandise to the above named individuals, after identifying the stolen items by

placing my initials thereon.

I certify that the above consent has been freely and voluntarily given by me

and that no threats or promises have been made to me.

I further agree that the above named individuals may enter the above described

premises to assist me in locating the stolen merchandise, and that I shall make no

claim whatsoever against the above named persons, (Company Name), its officers and

employees, in connection with the entry and search of the above premises and the

return of the stolen merchandise.

Date: _____

Witnesses: Signature: _____

_____

_____

Consent of Spouse, or Co-owner, or Proprietor of Premises:

I, _____, hereby consent to the entry of
(Name of person and relationship to employee or premises)

the above described premises by the above named individuals.

Date: _____

Witnesses: Signature: _____

_____

_____   APA - 1973 SAMPLE

Figure 9.5 Consent to search form.

the part of the spouse. This should not deter the search, as long as one of the spouses has consented to the search.

In most searches of this type, the investigator is almost totally dependent upon the suspect to identify the stolen merchandise so that its recovery can be effected. During the trip to the house and during the search, the suspect should be reminded that the complete procedure includes a polygraph test, if legal. He should be told several times that one of the questions will cover his cooperation in turning over all stolen property during the search. The thought of the polygraph test acts as a great mental prodder in encouraging the suspect to release all of the stolen goods.

In other words, the search is not a true search in the sense of a police-type operation. Nothing is going to be removed from the premises except that which is identified by the suspect as having been stolen. The only exception to this is merchandise in an original container that would clearly indicate that it was stolen, and where the container itself rules out the possibility of the merchandise ever having been obtained legally. In this case, without the suspect's cooperation, the investigator should make a seizure of the item and, of course, give the suspect a receipt.

The investigator should not attempt to search the home of a minor if the parents are present and refuse cooperation. If the parents are not home, then the investigator should confine the search to the minor's room in the home. Even in so doing, there is a risk of eventual lawsuit on the part of the parents, but many security directors consider this an acceptable risk.

Although many security agencies have expertise in interrogation and taking statements, a great number of them hesitate to pursue a case beyond that point, and in reality make little or no effort to effect a recovery of merchandise. Some security people are content simply to allow the suspect to "bring in the merchandise the next day." With this approach, all the merchandise may not be recovered, but it probably does reduce somewhat the risk of a lawsuit. It also reduces the risk of bodily injury to the investigator. Experience has shown that in an operation of this type, the most dangerous situation that can present itself occurs during the search of a suspect's home. Here, the chances of finding hidden weapons or belligerent relatives are all greatly increased. Unless an investigator is armed, it is not advisable for only one person to conduct house searches.

A female employee should play a key role in any subsequent search of a female suspect's home. Under no circumstances should a male investigator take a female suspect to her home alone, even though she has signed a Consent to Search form. She should be accompanied throughout the entire procedure by another female whose presence, once again, greatly deters the possibility of a later charge of impropriety against the investigator.

Once the stolen merchandise is recovered, it should be returned to the motel and processed in the waiting room. This can easily be done in front of the other suspects, and serves to act as a powerful preconditioner to their own interrogation or house searches. In processing the merchandise, the investigator can enlist the suspect's assistance in marking each item for identification. The entire inventory and marking of the items should be recorded on a Property Recovery sheet (Figure 9.6), which ultimately forms a permanent record of

PROPERTY RECOVERY SHEET   Page_____ of _____

The following is a list of property stolen by _____
(subject's name)

from _____ located at _____
(company name)   (company address)

and surrendered to/seized by _____ , _____
(circle one, cross out other)   (name)   (title)

at _____
(describe fully where recovery occurred)

at _____ on _____ .
(time)   (date)

SUBJECT: _____ POSITION: _____

ADDRESS: _____ CITY: _____ STATE: _____

WITNESSES TO SEARCH OR RECOVERY: (give names and addresses)

RECOVERY MADE BY:

☐ Search Warrant

☐ Consent to Search

☐ Voluntary Surrender

☐ _____
(other)

IDENTIFICATION MADE BY:

☐ Subject_____
(name)

☐ Sec. Off. _____

☐ Management _____

☐ _____
(other)

QUAN.	SIZE	AREA OF RECOVERY	DESCRIPTION OF ITEM/MERCHANDISE	UNIT PRICE	VALUE

"I have personally identified the above items/merchandise as being the property of _____
(company name)
and certify that this is an accurate record of this recovery. I have completed this form voluntarily and no promises or threats have been made to me." **WITNESS TO SIGNATURE:**

_____

_____   _____
(signature)

(date and time)

The above items/merchandise have been marked in the following manner:
_____
(describe fully how items/merchandise were marked)

_____
(signature of security officer)

Figure 9.6 Property recovery sheet.

how and under what circumstances the merchandise was recovered. Months or even years later it may become extremely important to know all the details surrounding the recovery of the merchandise, and especially any witnesses present. By proper use of the Property Recovery sheet, a permanent record is obtained, which can prove invaluable in any criminal proceedings that may later develop.

CHAPTER 10

ROLE OF THE POLYGRAPH AND DISPOSITION OF OFFENDERS

THE POLYGRAPH AND INVESTIGATION

Supportive Role

The ability to use polygraph examinations in conjunction with the overall efforts of the "bust" is highly desirable. It makes for a much more complete investigation. It is through the use of the polygraph that the true perspective of the case can be fully developed and management can be made aware of the full extent of their losses. The inability to utilize polygraph tests in this type of setting is not fatal to the company's investigative objectives, however. The polygraph's role is an ancillary one rather than a technique utilized in a first-line offensive.

In the first edition of this text, the author suggested the use of the polygraph in a supportive role, and at that time it was possible to do this without any restrictions. Although polygraphs can still be used in specific situations, there are now restrictions to be observed that have come about through the passage of the Employee Polygraph Protection Act (E.P.P.A.) of 1988. The E.P.P.A. is a restrictive law against polygraph that had long been pushed by organized labor and the American Civil Liberties Union. In 1988 this, along with one or two other minor measures, seemed to be the lesser of labor's demands to the Congress of the United States and consequently the law was passed and signed by President Reagan. The effective date of the law was set at December 27, 1988.

There are a number of provisions in the law that provide for exemptions on pre-employment testing, but this chapter will concern itself only with the observances that must be made by both management and polygraph examiners in utilizing the technique in specific cases. This section on polygraph is not meant to be definitive but rather to give senior security management and others general guidelines on what may be possible. For specific interpretation of the act, corporate security persons should refer to interpretations by their legal counsel.[16] The United States Department of Labor, specifically the Wage and Hour Division, has been charged by Congress with enactment of rules and regulations to administer the act. That government office has published tentative final rules in the Federal Register as of October 21, 1988. Although it is possible that there may be some minor changes to the rules, the major guidelines will undoubtedly remain. Some of the more important caveats of these rules are as follows:

1. Inventory shortages in and of themselves cannot be the basis for requesting specific polygraph examinations.
2. Any specific testing must be related to economic loss to the company and such economic loss in turn has to be related to 50 percent or more of the employer's business.

In other words, a company engaged in the manufacture of footwear that constitutes over 50 percent of their business, could not utilize polygraph for investigation of thefts from vending machines from the company lunchroom.

3. Notice to employees of the company's wish to administer polygraph tests must be given 48 hours in advance, not to include holiday and weekend days.
4. The polygraph examination must be part of an ongoing investigation of economic loss or injury to the company.
5. If a state law or collective bargaining agreement is more restrictive than the Federal anti-polygraph law, such state law or labor agreement prevails. If such item is less restrictive, then the E.P.P.A. prevails.

Specifically, then, the final tentative rules by the Department of Labor say that: (1) There must be an ongoing investigation. (2) The employee must have had access to the loss. (3) The employer must have a reasonable suspicion that a particular employee is involved in the incident or activity being investigated and this must be spelled out in a statement to the employee. (4) Such statements should also explain the economic loss to the company, the access by the employee, and *why reasonable* suspicion exists. This must

---

[16]The United States Chamber of Commerce, through its own legal section, has published guidelines for companies. A copy of questions and answers contained in these guidelines can be found in Appendix 4.

be signed by an official of the company and a copy of this document must be retained for three years.

Other points for employers to consider are that no random testing is possible and that the polygraph cannot be used to pry into drug and alcohol abuse, even where it may have played a role in the economic loss.

The government has declared "reasonable suspicion" cannot be defined as possible or potential opportunity only. It does concede that "reasonable suspicion" might be derived from information from a coworker or from employee behavior, demeanor, or conduct. In other words, as the author had proposed in the original edition of this book, if the polygraph is used to verify confessions already made, this meets the test of "reasonable suspicion." The government also concedes that there may be circumstances surrounding the access or opportunity that would meet the test of "reasonable suspicion."

One prominent polygraph company, John E. Reid and Associates, Inc., has developed a model set of forms with the help of their counsel Charles Marino of Chicago. These necessary notification and release forms are reproduced with their permission. (See Appendix 3.) When adapting these forms, security practitioners should obtain approval from their own legal counsel.

For all the above reasons, the polygraph's proper role in a large "bust" situation is that of a supportive investigative tool, one that must be integrated with the other investigative techniques utilized by the security director.

Proper Polygraph Applications

When utilized properly as a support tool in the "bust" situation, the polygraph technique has the principal role of verifying admissions and true total amounts of goods stolen, identifying co-offenders, and locating stolen goods. In the verification of admissions and true total amounts, the best time for a polygraph examination is following a house search but preceding a formal statement. In other words, no formal statement should be attempted unless the security director feels certain that all the information that can be developed on a particular suspect has been developed. There is one and only one way that this can be done, and that is through polygraph technique.

As a part of the general processing of an offender in a large group, it is customary that he be asked to sign a polygraph consent form some time after making an initial preliminary statement and prior to the house search.

The Verification Test

In any large "bust" situation, the following relevant questions should be included in the polygraph examination:

1. Do you know anyone stealing from _____ company? (optional)
2. Have you ever worked in collusion with anyone to steal merchandise from _____ company?
3. Have you stolen (any) more than _____ dollars in property from _____ company?
4. Have you ever sold any stolen _____ company property?
5. Do you know where any stolen _____ company property is located?

The above test questions are those most commonly used in a large-scale industrial theft investigation. Occasionally, the security director and the polygraph examiner may wish to resort to other more specialized tests.

Peak of Tension (P.O.T.) Tests

On occasion, an employee suspect may be encountered who will make some minor admissions of theft, but for one reason or another refuses to expand his admissions and give a true amount. Where the security director has reason to feel that this is the case, he may request the polygraphist to utilize a peak of tension test designed to pinpoint the total amounts of theft.

A basic example is a case in which a suspect has made an admission of approximately ten dollars; the question range starts with one dollar, and then five dollars, and continues on up into the hundreds or even thousands, as the case may be. Most polygraphists then prefer to come back down the scale in reverse order. If the examinee is properly prepared psychologically, the polygraphist will usually be able to pinpoint the general area of the true amount of his thefts. Although this certainly is not conclusive from the standpoint of winning an arbitration or a prosecution, it has a very beneficial effect on the suspect and is a great aid to an interrogator who may wish to attempt further questioning.

Basically the same type of test, although of a more probing nature, can be used to identify co-offenders and also the location of hidden contraband.

Properly used, then, the polygraph can be of great assistance in the overall investigation. It also plays an important role in the disposition of offenders and rehabilitation of employees, if this is to become a factor.

DISPOSITION OF OFFENDERS

The Decision to Retain or Discharge

In any large theft investigation, management is often faced with a final decision as to who should be separated from the payroll and who should be retained. If the investigation was widespread, identifying many of the employees as engaging in dishonest acts, management may be forced to make a business decision based on a desire to keep the facility in operation. In many cases, it would be foolhardy to discharge each and every admitted thief, as there would not be sufficient trained personnel remaining to keep the company's business going. Therefore, the decision comes down to where to draw the line.

If there is a union in the picture, management must be circumspect in drawing such a line so that they do not deviate from their own standards and are consistent in applying them uniformly. If the facility is not unionized, management has the prerogative to discharge whomever it wishes and, conversely, to retain any persons deserving of such retention.

By studying the security director's control sheet, management should be able to determine at what point a reasonable cut-off line can be drawn. It is not practicable here to attempt to suggest any definite dollar amount of theft that should be grounds for discharge, as all amounts must be relative from one case to another. That is, in some cases amounts of admitted theft in the area of two to four hundred dollars might very well be considered minor, whereas in other investigations, minor amounts might be considered to be those less than fifty dollars.

The security director, however, should attempt to dissuade management from retaining any persons who have been unable to verify their own admissions through polygraph; that is, those whose confessions could not be verified as being complete. Also to be excluded from any consideration of rehabilitation should be those persons admitting the sale of company property, regardless of the amount involved. To put it another way, only those offending employees who have admitted minor amounts of pilferage for their own personal or their family's use, who have not engaged in selling stolen merchandise, and who have been able to verify that their admission is complete through polygraph examination, should be considered worthy of retention. The company must be prepared, however, to clearly state what those conditions are that influence the discharge of the other offenders. If they are consistent in adhering to the standards that they themselves set up, the company should be successful in gaining the support of any labor arbitrator.

In regard to those who are retained, it is beneficial to be able to show an arbitrator that such retention has its own conditions—namely restitution by payroll deduction.

Larceny Charges

Regardless of any desire on the part of management to prosecute, many larceny cases never find their way into the criminal justice system. When they do, the most common charge is larceny, but that very charge carries with it certain complications that reduce overall the number of thefts referred to the police or district attorney. The main complication arising in a larceny case is that of the proof of the *corpus delecti*. This literally means the body of the crime. In any criminal proceedings, it is absolutely essential that the prosecution first prove that a crime was, in fact, committed. The next step is to prove who did it. For this reason, confessions in and of themselves are insufficient to win criminal prosecution.

The burden of proof of the *corpus delecti* rests upon the prosecution and not upon the defense. An inventory shortage is insufficient to establish a *corpus delecti*, although it can be a part of the ingredients of the *corpus delecti*, if other facts are there to support it. The *corpus delecti* can often be shown in a number of ways, such as breaking and entering, eyewitness testimony, or even the recovery of stolen company property.

Identifying Stolen Property

If recovered company property is to be used in establishing the *corpus delecti*, then the prosecution has the burden of showing that the property in question can be positively identified as stolen property, and that the defendant could not have come into possession of such property in any legal manner. Once again, the burden of proving this rests upon the prosecution and not the defense. In other words, the defendant does not have to prove that he came into possession of the property legally, but rather the prosecution has to show that he could not possibly have come into possession of the property legally.

The following case history illustrates the painstaking efforts that can go into proving the *corpus delecti*.

Long Island City, New York. After many months of surveillance of a liquor warehouse, the investigation team concluded that a shop steward on the night shift was utilizing his personal automobile to remove cases of Scotch whisky from the warehouse. Surveillance had established a regular pattern of deliveries to various customers in the borough of Brooklyn. In order to be able to prove that there was no chance that the subject could have purchased the cases of whisky, the investigators were forced to go to great lengths to make the problem of the *corpus delecti* airtight.

Inasmuch as it had been planned to intercept the shop steward on a Monday morning while he was making his deliveries of whisky, the investigators spent all of Sunday inside the warehouse, marking certain brands of Scotch whisky so that positive identification could be made the following morning if the apprehension were successful. This task was enormous, as there were hundreds and hundreds of cases to be marked in such a way as not to alert the shop steward.

As events later proved, when the steward and the night crew reported at midnight on Sunday night for work, the shop steward loaded six of the marked cases into the trunk of his automobile, which he had parked inside the building. When the apprehension was made, there was no problem in identifying the six cases and eliminating even the remote possibility that he could have purchased the six cases on his way to work that evening.

Other Charges

Occasionally, when the security manager finds that proving the *corpus delecti* is an insurmountable task, he may find that he is able to prosecute on the basis of conspiracy. In a conspiracy, it is not necessary to prove that a crime was committed. It is only necessary to prove that two or more persons conspired to commit the crime and that at least one overt act was performed towards that commission. In a theft ring situation, this often can be proved through the testimony of one of the conspirators, or possibly even an undercover agent.

In some states, the charge of embezzlement is applicable even though it may not involve a company accountant or the actual financial records of the firm. Basically, embezzlement is a charge that applies when someone who is entrusted with the custody of the goods absconds with same, as opposed to a larcenous person who may merely have access to the stolen goods. In a true embezzlement, the proof of the *corpus delecti* is usually much easier than in a larceny case, as the altered financial records of the company become, in fact, the body of the crime.

Other charges that may be available to the security director in order to make his case are drug violations and, of course, gambling charges. Here, the recovery of illicit drugs or gambling paraphernalia automatically constitutes the *corpus delecti*, and from there the prosecution may proceed to show, through confessions or other evidence, who the perpetrators of such crimes were.

Many security authorities feel that a certain percentage of employee crimes should be prosecuted, as prosecution has a therapeutic effect on the rest of the work force. Failure to prosecute simply means that the severest penalty to be encountered is loss of one's job. This is a small price to pay for the professional industrial thief who goes from job to job in order to rip off his employers and, in effect, make the majority of his income from a life of crime.

SECTION IV

Making the Company Whole

CHAPTER 11

RECOVERY PROCEDURES

Having accomplished his primary objective of separating thieves from the payroll, the security director should turn his attention toward attempts to make recoveries on behalf of the company and also toward instituting procedures and controls that will act as a future deterrent to a repetition of the dishonesty. New security procedures and controls are more easily accepted by management following a major investigation than at any other time. The security manager can and should follow the old adage of "striking while the iron is hot."

On the other hand, very often recovery attempts will become quite involved and almost as time-consuming as certain phases of the original investigation. Many thieves will readily accept their discharge from the company and even bow to prosecution by a plea of guilty, but will rebel when pressure is brought to make a substantial financial recovery, which could easily involve all of the offender's assets.

RESTITUTION

In many major investigations, a management decision to keep some of the lesser offenders on the payroll may be a prudent one. Often, to separate all of the offenders from the company means crippling company operations and is entirely counterproductive. For those offenders who are retained on the payroll, it must be understood by all parties that restitution in a mutually agreeable amount is imperative.

Negotiations

On the question of restitution, it must be kept in mind that in most theft cases, the amounts of theft recorded, even in the best of confessions, are often estimates. For this reason, the exact amount of restitution should be negotiable between the director of security and the offender. The personnel department of the company should normally sit in on such negotiations, but the actual negotiations should be conducted by the security chief and no one else. To turn the matter of negotiated restitution over to the personnel department, or to some third person who was never a party to the investigation or the confession, is ill advised. It will only result in an unrealistic amount being demanded or agreed upon.

The main thrust of any negotiation regarding restitution is to insure that there is complete understanding among all parties that restitution is not being asked or given as a trade-off to criminal prosecution. The company should make clear that any restitution is clearly in recognition of the offending employee's civil obligation and not any criminal liability that he may possess.

As a practical matter, however, most prosecutors would never entertain the thought of prosecuting an employee once the company had entered into a restitution agreement. The only question of immunity at this point is that of immunity against loss of the offender's job. A suggested form for restitution from retained offenders is shown in Figure 11.1.

In the case of persons who are prosecuted, occasionally overtures will be made to the company by the offender or a close relative to accept restitution prior to the case coming to trial. If such an overture is received, it should be reported immediately to the prosecutor, and no acceptance of the offer should be made without the prosecutor's full blessing. Because of future relations with the police and prosecuting attorney, it is a grave mistake for a company to accept money from an offender in a unilateral action.

If money is to be accepted at all under these circumstances, it should be accepted in whole and never in part. The company should take the position that it is not a collection agency and should demand payment in full, leaving the burden of financing the obligation up to the offender.

The Promissory Note

Occasionally, in isolated cases, the security director will realize that a significant and substantial amount of money can be acquired through the recovery process prior to even making contact with the prosecutor's office. In these cases, it is suggested that a promissory note, such as is shown in Figure 11.2, be signed by the offender. In utilizing such a note, the security official should insert a rate of interest in order that the note be legally binding. The company should further take the position that payment of the note must be made within several days, and in full.

CONSENT TO RESTITUTION

I, _____, confirm the previous statement (s)

dated _____, acknowledging thefts of property of_____

_____, and to the best of my knowledge, the total

amount of_____ property that I have stolen is $_____.

I further confirm my wish to reimburse_____, for

the value of the property that I have stolen, and I hereby promise to pay the sum

of $_____ @ the rate of_____. I further

authorize _____, to withhold such sum from my salary,

applying the amount so withheld in reduction of this obligation.

It is understood that this acknowledgement of my obligation and promise to

repay, is made solely in recognition of my civil obligation to_____

_____,and that no promises of immunity from prosecution

have been made to me by_____, or its officers or

agents.

Date:_____   Signed:_____

Witnessed:

_____

_____

Figure 11.1 Suggested form for restitution from offenders who are retained as employees.

Here again, the problem of raising the money for financing of the obligation is left entirely to the offender and/or his relatives. If a cash settlement is offered by a relative, the company should not accept it as such. Instead, the company should demand that the money be advanced to the offender and payment of the funds made directly by the offender to the company.

NOTE

$ ....   Date .... , ...

On demand, for value received, I ....

promise to pay to .... , or order,

the sum of .... Dollars

in lawful money of the United States, with interest at the rate of .... per cent per annum, interest payable monthly.

In case said interest is not paid when due, it shall be added to the principal and bear a like rate of interest until paid and the whole of said principal and interest shall forthwith become due at the option of the holder hereof without notice.

All sums shall be paid at ....

The consideration for this note is money owed by me to .... and is not given in exchange for any promise, express or implied, to withhold or stifle criminal prosecution.

In case suit is brought to collect this note or any portion thereof I promise and agree to pay such additional sum as the court may adjudge reasonable for attorneys' fees in said action.

Witness ....   Address ....

Figure 11.2   Promissory note to be signed by offender.

As with a restitution agreement, the vast majority of prosecuting attorneys never accept a case in which a promissory note has been rendered and payment made. The security director should keep in mind, however, that in many states it is mandatory to report a felony that has been committed. Although this law is seldom enforced, especially in the context of industrial theft losses, the security chief should be aware that technically he could be compounding a felony by accepting restitution and failing to report the felony to proper authorities.

As stated above, the company should demand payment in full. It is an old tactic for an offender to come in, for example, with an offer of one thousand dollars cash on a five thousand dollar obligation. Psychologically, he is banking on the fact that the security chief will accept the thousand dollars in hand. The offender realizes that once any part of the restitution has been accepted, he has very little to worry about, practically speaking, in the way of prosecution. It then becomes a struggle for the company to effect collection of the other four thousand dollars.

Another good use to which the promissory note can be put is in the presentation of a bonding claim, which will be discussed later in this chapter.

Restitution

Where the security chief feels that the offender has assets that can be converted in order to liquidate the obligation, or where he anticipates problems in effecting a collection, he may wish to take his chances on a strong prosecution in the criminal justice procedure.

In the case of first offenders and many second-time offenders, the courts will often order restitution as a condition of probation. The security director has to be extremely cautious not to make it appear that he is simply using the prosecutor's office and the courts as a collection agency. In other words, he should take the position that his primary interest is in furthering justice, and that any restitution that may be obtained through the probation is only secondary. As a practical matter, however, the entire criminal justice procedure can often work to the benefit of the injured company.

Civil Suits

After the smoke has cleared from the battlefield of discharge and prosecutions, the company may wish to entertain the thought of recovery through civil court action. Many states have come to recognize the problem of industrial theft, and a few have passed statutes for up to treble damages in such instances. Civil suits are easily undertaken and involve little or no risk to the company. They are best handled by a lawyer who specializes in collections. Such an attorney is a much better choice than ordinary corporate counsel, as he will normally work on a percentage of the recovery. Often the only costs to the company are filing fees.

Seldom do the offenders force such issues to go into full-blown court proceedings. Experience has shown that most of these actions result in default judgments, which then become routine collection matters for the company's attorney. Here again, of course, the existence of a promissory note or good formal statement enhances the attorney's negotiating position. In actions of this type, the recovery efforts are usually stretched out over many years, but they are handled by the attorney and require little or no attention from corporate officials.

THE BONDING CLAIM

Potential Problems

Of all the different recovery options open to a corporation, the one that can sometimes prove the most troublesome is the bonding claim.

The settlement of a bonding claim can produce much misunderstanding and ill feeling between the company and its insurance carrier, simply because the company does not have a clear understanding of the insurance carrier's role when such a claim is presented.

In regular crime coverage by an insurance company, such as burglary and robbery insurance, the carrier is insuring the company against the stated risks. When an incident occurs, it is usually a matter of official record and there is little or no question regarding the happening. Claims of this type usually are settled promptly, without question, and with residual good feelings on the part of both participants.

In fidelity insurance, the role of the bonding company becomes somewhat different. Although the fidelity bond itself is bought and paid for by the company, the insurance carrier takes the posture that it is, in effect, insuring the employees of the company against defalcations. This concept is different from that in which the insurance carrier is insuring the company against an outside threat.

Most insurance carriers in the past twenty years have found the fidelity bond business to be generally unprofitable and refuse to write such insurance, unless they feel compelled to do so in order to retain other profitable insurance coverage purchased by the company. In defense of the insurance carriers, it must be pointed out that there have been instances where companies have attempted to use fidelity bond claims to recoup losses suffered through mysterious disappearances, general inventory shortages, and the like. Some security persons have also been guilty of unscrupulous and unethical practices in securing inflated confessions from employees, only to attempt to make money for the company at the insurance carrier's expense.

Normally the insurance carrier is not a party to the closing of a major investigation, nor should it be. It must be kept in mind that it is in the insurance carrier's interest to hold down the amounts of the confessions, whereas, of course, it is in the interest of the security chief to develop the confessions to their fullest extent.

In other words, the bonding claim is the end product of efforts expended by the company, without any collaboration or consultation with the insurance carrier, to obtain a cash settlement from the carrier under the terms of the bond. For this and other reasons stated above, most insurance carriers are initially cool and unhelpful when such a claim is received. They tend to enter negotiations on such a claim from an adversary position rather than that of a cooperative partnership with the company in resolving the problem at hand.

Factors Influencing Settlement

Few, if any, bonding claims have ever been settled on one hundred percent of face value; rather, they are settled on a percentage of the total claim. Such percentage is usually determined through many negotiating sessions, and is influenced to a great extent by the strength of the security director's case. In other words, the stronger the claim, the higher the settlement.

Inventory Records. Most fidelity insurance policies are clear in pointing out that no bonding claim will be accepted on the basis of a shortage in inventory records. On the other hand, once the claim has been made and accepted by the bonding company, the security director can utilize inventory records to bolster his case. Conversely, a bonding company reviewing and negotiating such a claim will almost always ask for inventory records, and if these are not supportive of the claim, the net result is a weakening of the company's overall position. Stated another way, inventory records cannot be utilized as the basis for a claim, but will ultimately serve either to enhance or detract from the security director's negotiating position.

Production Records. Although almost all fidelity policies have the standard prohibition against utilizing inventory records as a basis for a claim, many are silent when it comes to production records, and it may be that a company's production records can very well become the basis of a bonding claim.

Accounting Records. Accounting records, unlike inventory or production records, are generally irrefutable. In a bonding claim based on an embezzlement, the accounting records can serve as the entire basis of the claim itself, even without a confession.

Undercover Investigation. Most astute claim adjusters will raise the question of undercover efforts early in the negotiating process. They will wish to obtain the entire story of the investigation, and if undercover was utilized, they will demand copies of the undercover reports. The security director has little choice in this matter; refusal to release the reports only weakens his negotiating position.

On the other hand, a favorite tactic of most bonding companies is to take the position, based on the undercover reports, that any thefts that occurred after the initial discoveries by the undercover agent cannot be included in the claim. This is based on the standard clause in most bonding contracts that once a theft is discovered by the employer, the employee is no longer bonded, and the insurance company is no longer financially liable for any acts resulting from that time on.

There are two negotiating positions the security chief can take in rebuttal to this posture by the insurance company: 1) that the undercover agent's reports were not available to management until the conclusion of the investigation; 2) that it was only reasonable for the company to wish to identify all the thieves rather than precipitate a premature exposure of only one or two.

If the amount of thefts that occurred after the undercover agent's initial efforts is significant, the company may have to resort to pressure, through its insurance broker, on a higher level of management within the insurance carrier. This can often be accomplished if the insurance carrier is providing other forms of insurance for the company and its relationship with the company can be viewed in an overall context rather than just on the basis of fidelity bonding coverage.

Here again, as in the case of inventory records, undercover reports can serve to bolster the claim but at the same time can often reduce the size of the claim if the carrier is successful in eliminating a significant number of thefts from the total.

Arbitration and Court Findings. A successful labor arbitration ruling or a guilty finding by a criminal court will greatly bolster the bonding claim. On the other hand, a not-guilty finding by a criminal court will weaken the claim. An adverse ruling by a labor arbitrator simply makes the bonding claim a moot question, as the offender is usually back on the payroll at that point.

Validity of Confession. With the possible exception of some embezzlement cases, the central core of any bonding claim will be the confession and how much weight should be attached to its validity. All the records and reports involved in the foregoing discussion generally tend to support or strengthen the weight of the confession, but, on the other hand, if sufficient thought is not given to them beforehand, they sometimes can be used to subtract from the strength of the confession in supporting a claim.

Before starting negotiations with the insurance carrier, management should realize that the negotiating tactics of the claims adjuster will be to cast doubt on the validity of the confession, especially on the amounts of merchandise and/or money specified in such a statement. The more doubt that can be cast in this direction, the less money will be paid by the carrier to the company.

As a rule of thumb, a good handwritten statement by an offender, with little or no supporting evidence, is worth fifty cents on the dollar at best. In many cases it will be worth less than that. On the other hand, a good typewritten formal statement (question-and-answer style) with an impressive chain of supporting facts such as undercover reports, successful prosecution, inventory records, etc., is worth somewhere around seventy-five to eighty cents on the dollar. If management realizes this before even starting negotiations, their overall attitude and relationship with the insurance carrier will be on a much more amicable plane when the negotiations are concluded.

Deductibles

In virtually all fidelity bond policies there is a deductible clause. In computing the mathematics of the settlement, it is imperative that the deductible be applied to the total claim prior to any discounting of confessions. In all probability, the total claim will be based on amounts stated in written confessions by the offending employees. If these confessions are discounted, as discussed above, before the deductible is applied, the deductible will be reducing a lesser claim than the original claim. Therefore, it is in the interests of the company to have the deductible applied initially and resist any attempts by the adjuster to apply the deductible after a discounted amount has been agreed upon in relation to the confessions.

Most policies provide that the deductible is based on a per person involvement except where there is a collusive effort. In other words, where five employees have stolen separately and independently of each other, five deductibles would be applied to the total claim. On the other hand, if four of the five acted in concert and in collusion with each other, then only two deductibles would be applied; if all five were involved in a common theft ring, then only one deductible would be applied.

This points up the desirability and the necessity for developing complete information in any corroborative statements by co-offenders. This is one of the reasons why co-offenders should be present during the taking of formal statements and should sign as witnesses to each other's signatures on their respective statements. It becomes increasingly difficult for a bonding company to attempt to discount a confession when four other offenders have made essentially the same confession and corroborated in almost every detail each other's involvement.

Bonding Company's Recovery Attempts

After the settlement of the claim, the bonding companies almost always attempt recovery efforts of their own. This is normally referred to as "salvage." Under the terms of most bonding contracts, the bonding company is obligated to attempt to make a recovery on behalf of the employer, but only after satisfying their own reimbursement for moneys paid out in settlement of the bonding claim. In other words, the bonding company must be paid first, and if there is anything left over it goes to the employer. By the same token, if the security director has been successful in obtaining even partial restitution from one or more of the offenders who are included in the bonding claim, such recovery must be shown as a credit in computing the final settlement of the claim.

Premium Increases

It is the practice of most insurance carriers who write fidelity bond insurance to raise the premiums or the deductibles, or both, following the payment of claims. When the time for renewal of a policy arrives, the insurance company will review its experience with the particular company and, based on such experience, will raise the premium and/or deductible, or possibly leave it unchanged if no claims have been submitted. Knowing the realities of the situation, many company financial officers have taken the position that bonding insurance should only be utilized for a true catastrophe, and that routine bonding claims based on the efforts of the security department should not be put forward to the insurance company.

However, if a company has never submitted a bonding claim in the past and has continually paid bonding insurance premiums over a long period of years, there is no question but that the bonding company has made a substantial amount of money in writing the bond. Based on the premise that an efficient and progressive security department can ultimately clean up most thievery in a corporation, it is the author's opinion that most bonding claim issues should be submitted, even though they precipitate increased deductibles and/ or premiums. Eventually the deductibles will reach a level where the insurance truly becomes catastrophe insurance, but by then most of the routine thievery should have been cleaned up in the company and this high deductible will have little impact.

Prolonged Negotiations

A final note that corporate officials should keep in mind when pursuing a bonding claim is that the bonding company will automatically set up a financial reserve for a realistic maximum on the case. This is done at the time that the "proof of loss" is first submitted to the insurance carrier. From that point on, it is in the interests of the bonding company to drag out negotiations on the settlement for as long as possible, because, in effect, they are operating on money that has already been earmarked for the corporation in question rather than for themselves and, of course, is interest-free. By improving their cash flow in this manner, the insurance carrier can thus reduce short-term borrowings at the prevailing prime rate. It is believed that this policy is followed by the majority of major fidelity bond underwriters, and is one of a number of reasons why it becomes difficult to effect a speedy settlement of a bonding claim. Of course, if the final settlement reached is below the maximum amount of the reserve that had been set up, the difference reverts back to the insurance carrier as an added profit.

In conclusion, it is clear that a major responsibility of a security director is to effect financial recoveries for his company whenever possible. Obviously, he has a number of options, but it is just as obvious that he must be well versed in the various strategies and legalities that are involved in any of these processes.

Employee Relations

It is generally conceded that the vast majority of American employees prefer to work in an atmosphere free of theft, drug abuse, or other criminal violations.

Although the bulk of honest employees welcome and applaud their employer for removing hard-core thieves from the payroll, the process of removal is nevertheless traumatic on the work force as a whole. Therefore, the first order of business once the investigation itself is complete is for management to get the company productive again and the employees settled down in their jobs. One of the best ways to do this is in an employee meeting where management explains what has happened during the investigation, even though the explanation may be necessarily brief because of pending legal considerations. A suggested talk to the employees is reproduced from one used numerous times by a major American corporation.

Talk to Employees

During the last few days we have all been through some very trying and nerve-racking circumstances. I am happy to report that, to the best of my knowledge, the investigation which has been taking place has been concluded.

Many of you were interviewed during the investigation. I am happy that all of you who were interviewed have been cleared to return to work—on the other hand—some of our employees have been terminated because of facts that developed during the investigation. So you might say that the cancer has been removed. It is now time for all of us to work together to get back on a normal basis as quickly as possible and to see that the cancer is never permitted to root again.

During the last few years we have done our best to keep you informed of matters that concern you, which of course, include the progress of this Division. As you all know, our record has not been satisfactory. A company like ours cannot make satisfactory progress with the type of operation that we have had in our warehouse during the past year. With your cooperation we can now change the direction in which we have been going and make this Division a good place for honest people to work.

In reviewing the facts developed during the investigation, it seems that one of the major problems was a lack of attention to Company Rules. This was the root of the evil that existed. Violators of rules, who were not punished, soon lost respect for themselves, the Company and their fellow employees. They committed offenses far more serious than rule violations. Naturally, they were discovered and paid a high price—the loss of their jobs.

Sometimes employees regard rules as being sort of a strait-jacket, imposed on them by the management just for management's protection—this is not the case in our business. In our Employee Handbook (hold up a copy) we say here on page ———:

> "These rules are designed not only for the safekeeping of Company merchandise and other property, but also to *protect our employees* from innocently engaging in practices that may result in their dismissal and possible prosecution."

As brought out previously, some time ago we had a meeting and discussed with you the subject of Company rules and the importance of security in our business. The topic of my talk was "Security Is Everybody's Business". At that time we reviewed our rules, distributed copies of them to all employees and posted them on our bulletin boards. We did this because there is so much at stake—and the consequences of violating these rules are so tragic that we wanted to make sure that you knew and understood them and what would happen if they are not strictly observed.

As I said before, we have just gone through an unfortunate and sad experience and it has been a trial for all of us. We here in this room are fortunate that we do not have to suffer the consequences as those who were involved in this sorrowful affair.

Let me say that I have confidence in those of you who remain and earnestly hope that you will follow our rules and cooperate with management in its program of rule enforcement. It is only through this means that we can help our people protect themselves.

Now I would like to be doubly sure that you know and understand our rules. I will review the more important ones with you again, so that if there are questions, they may be cleared up now."

CHAPTER 12

POST-OPERATIVE THERAPY

Having made recovery efforts for his company, the security director should not consider his task complete until he has laid the groundwork and instituted programs for the future, programs designed to reduce the chance of a repetition of the "illness" his company has just endured.

Many corporate security departments are oriented toward investigative procedures and little else. Over the years, they have developed excellent expertise in investigative technique and established outstanding track records for the apprehension of dishonest employees. However, their task is a never-ending one as they simply go from one major investigation to another. On the other hand, other corporate security departments have been noted for their strong approach to preventive and control procedures, with little emphasis and almost no expertise in the field of investigation. A disproportionate reliance on either approach, by itself, does not work in the best interests of the corporation.

Enlightened security management, and even corporate management as a whole, will recognize and accept the fact that good selection procedures and internal controls are basically designed for honest people—those in the center of the spectrum whose propensities toward dishonesty or honesty can go either way. This same enlightened thinking will also accept the fact that if a company has confirmed, hard-core thieves on its payroll, normal security controls and procedures will not deter the hard-core element from thievery unless the company is prepared to operate a penitentiary. The controls will, ironically, cause the thieves to become even more adept in their efforts and more difficult to apprehend.

In other words, controls are only as good as the people who administer them, and when the "people factor" is taken into consideration, one immediately must recognize the existence of human weaknesses and human error. Thieves recognize this, and wait for the opportunity to take advantage of any weakness or loophole. Therefore, the correct approach to the whole problem of industrial and business security is a blending of the two—investigation and controls. The correct proportions of the blend will be determined largely by the nature of the company's business and the make-up of its work force.

APPLICANT SCREENING AND EMPLOYEE SELECTION

It is absolutely essential in building a healthy company to begin with the selection of persons who are inherently honest, or at least basically honest if the proper controls and procedures are in effect. Hiring persons who have a history of consistent employee theft only insures that security problems will continue to develop and that there will always be plenty of work to occupy the investigation section of the security department.

Reference Check Limitations

Much has been written about the desirability of obtaining sufficient references on prospective employees. The plain truth of the matter is that seldom do such reference checks reveal any history of dishonesty. One reason is that most employee dishonesty goes undiscovered and is simply absorbed into the company's business; it is ultimately passed along to the consumer in the form of higher prices. Another reason is that, unfortunately, most employers are reluctant to release derogatory information about former employees out of fear of lawsuits. Consequently, employers have come to put little faith in the traditional reference letters because they themselves refuse to be candid in responding when such questionnaires reach their own desks.

In addition, America has experienced great shifts in population since World War II; ours has become a mobile society. Job applicants no longer generally come from an employer's immediate community; thus the employer must seek some method of screening prospective employees.

Most police departments and the FBI do not make their criminal files available to the private employer. This has come about because of the federal Privacy Act, as well as administrative prohibitions on police departments imposed by the Law Enforcement Assistance Administration. Many companies have found that the background investigation conducted by some private agencies often reveals little that is not already known to the employer. This especially holds true where the employer is paying minimal fees for such an investigation. Such investigations are particularly susceptible to influence by malicious neighbors, vindictive past employers, or disgruntled former fellow workers. Clearly, such a procedure is inadequate from the employer's view; equally important, it is fraught with the danger of injustice to the job applicant.

As is discussed in Chapter 7, high-quality background investigations can be very meaningful if the company is prepared to pay for such work. Such an investigation is conducted through field work and personal interviews. It is not conducted by telephone, and its cost may well exceed $400.00.

Polygraph as a Screening Tool

With the advent of the Employee Polygraph Protection Act (E.P.P.A.) of 1988, the vast majority of employers will no longer be able to use polygraph to screen job applicants.

Exemptions were made in E.P.P.A. for certain areas such as the drug industry, public power and transportation industries, and certain types of security industry jobs (specific security guard assignments).

The estimated one to two million job screening tests seen in the last few years will no longer be possible. In fact, McKesson Corporation, the oldest national polygraph user (since 1954) with one of the largest nation-wide screening endeavors, dropped its polygraph program in December 1988 after 34 years of successful operation. Although exempted under E.P.P.A., the company undoubtedly viewed the law as being so restrictive that it will eventually eliminate the supply of qualified polygraph practitioners necessary to maintain such a successful venture.

Written Honesty Tests

In those jurisdictions where pre-employment polygraphing is not possible due to legal restrictions, or even in remote areas where polygraph services are not available, a company should seriously consider the use of a paper-and-pencil honesty test on job applicants. As in polygraph testing, written honesty tests should normally be restricted to those persons having access to money or merchandise.

There are a number of good tests on the market, such as the Reid Report.[17] Most authorities in the field believe that there is no equal to a good polygraph pre-employment test, but that a paper-and-pencil honesty attitude test is a good possible substitute. The

---

[17]See footnote 1, Introduction, page 4.

publishers of the Reid Report claim to have a more extensive track record than other written honesty tests in various kinds of legal proceedings concerning the suitability of the report. They further claim that their product has undergone close scrutiny by various human rights commissions and the E.E.O.C. and has met the challenge. On a dollar-for-dollar basis, there is no question but that the written honesty test is a viable alternative if polygraph is illegal or unavailable.

The In-Depth Interview

Since the passage of the E.P.P.A., many polygraph examiners have begun offering clients the in-depth interview, also called the structured interview. On occasion, it is offered in combination with a written honesty test. Some security practitioners feel that this combination is the best substitute for the now nearly impossible polygraph screening test.

The in-depth interview has been a tool of polygraphists for 30 years or more, especially where a client did not favor the polygraph test or it was restricted by state law. It depends almost completely on the skill of the interviewer and utilizes kinesics, the art of reading body language. Obviously, polygraph examiners who were excellent interrogators with the polygraph will probably be able to develop and hold a viable clientele (those who give repeat business) in this regard.

Prices for this procedure alone will probably be slightly more than polygraph rates due to the added time for interviewing and preparation of the report.

INTERNAL CONTROLS

Internal controls almost invariably come about because of the dishonest activities of company employees. Probably ninety percent of all internal controls in existence today in any company can be traced to an incident of dishonesty in that company or in some other firm. In other words, if all employees were inherently honest, there would be no controls and companies would never give a second thought to internal security measures.

Within the scope of this text, it would be impossible to detail the type of controls that should be set up for any particular company. Controls will vary from corporation to corporation and will be based largely on the company's security history, lessons learned from other corporations, and the nature of the company's business.

While the amount of the paperwork portion of internal controls will have to be in balance with efficiency and cost, internal controls act as a strong deterrent to employee theft. Not only is there a psychological barrier raised, but the paperwork also helps provide an audit trail for company investigators. To keep internal controls at an effective level, they should be tested frequently by management or security personnel, e.g., "extra" merchandise added to a driver's load; "special" shipments into the company's own receiving department, where no purchase order is being held; an executive's attempt to circumvent normal house order procedures to test employee awareness. Finally, management should conduct an ongoing routine program of investigation of shortages or other irregularities. Such a program mentally reinforces the concept of controls in the employees' minds and creates the most important realization of all— management *does* care.

Security Inspection Check Lists

To give the reader an idea of the type of monitoring that should be done during a security inspection or a survey, a Security Inspection Report for apparel manufacturing locations is shown in Appendix 1. A similar form for use in a retail environment is also presented in Appendix 2. Many security managers will be quick to realize that additional points could be added to either of the forms presented. However, it must be remembered that a different type of company has different needs.

The important thing to note is that the questions are designed to get the inspector thinking in depth about the various logical security areas of the company's operations. Additionally, if the inspector will attempt to think beyond each question itself, and consider the question's *intent*, he will be able to formulate additional questions of his own. In this way, he may uncover weaknesses that would not be spotlighted by a person merely adhering to the printed format.

The reader will also note that both checklists start with questions on the personnel function. If the security department has been given sufficient latitude, certain personnel procedures should be included for the simple reason that good security begins with the selection of job applicants who are basically honest.

A well-done security inspection provides one additional dividend for the security manager—a future intelligence reference for overt and covert investigators.

Employee Education and Motivation

One nationally known security consultant has consistently maintained that company security departments should attempt to win over at least one-third of the employees in the battle against employee dishonesty. He has further stated that if as many as fifty percent of the employee work force can be converted to the side of security and honesty, then the war against employee theft has been won.

Opinions of other experts on these percentages and their ultimate effects vary, but generally all are in agreement that a certain number of the employees must be won over in order to make the security department's job meaningful. This can be done in a variety of ways, such as posters, pay envelope inserts, reward programs, and face-to-face meetings.

Experience has shown that it is generally easy for security department personnel to address employee groups on the question of dishonesty and its full ramifications, including its effects on the employee's family. It must be pointed out, however, that there is usually reluctance on the part of regular management to discuss matters of honesty and dishonesty with the rank-and-file employees. This is nothing more than a morale problem on the part of management people. They should be helped to understand that when it comes to matters of stealing, breaking the rules, breaking the law on company property, and other security violations, the employees themselves are quick to discuss these things at every given opportunity. Realizing this, security personnel have found it easy to have face-to-face talks with employee groups. For the same reason, it should be easy for management to do likewise. The need for education thus applies to management as well as to regular employees.

In locations where the employee work force is so great in numbers as to make such meetings impossible, monthly safety/security meetings can be instituted. In many companies utilizing the safety/security committee concept, members of the committee representing the rank-and-file employees are rotated every two or three months so that eventually a good cross-section of the employee work force has had some contact, either direct or indirect, with the security committee.

Employee education should be viewed as a never-ending process and one that is necessary in order to ultimately develop the degree of motivation that is desirable with the employee work force.

The Role of Management in Cooperation

No security program can ever be effective unless it has the complete backing of top management personnel. There probably always will be some members of middle management, as well as certain segments of the employee work force, who will automatically be anti-security. For this reason, it is imperative that any security program adopted has the backing of the most senior members of management in the corporation.

Many people in management today regard it as somewhat immoral if temptation is constantly placed in front of employees without necessary restraints and controls accompanying it. They further believe that the company has an obligation to its honest employees to help them remain honest, and that to turn away from this obligation is to be unfaithful to their employees as well as their own moral principles as professional managers. In some companies, senior management personnel have adopted an even more pragmatic viewpoint toward security, either in addition to the above or in place of it—namely, that the security department should be considered in the same light as any other profit center and that it has the capability of putting profits back onto the bottom line of the company's profit-and-loss statement that would be otherwise lost.

There is no question that the private security industry, as a whole, has as much if not more potential to affect the economy of the country and the entire cost of living on a day-to-day basis than the remainder of the whole criminal justice system.

Within management and the private security industry there must be a recognition that, despite good planning procedures, controls, and screening, there will always be a small element of the work force dedicated to theft or "ripping off the boss." Because of this, there will always be a need for good investigating capability. The modern day private enterprise system is too complex to think otherwise. Employee or internal theft must be investigated and exposed in order that overall progress in the war against internal crime be continued.

CHAPTER 13

INVESTIGATION OF SUSPECTED FRAUD AND MALINGERING IN WORKERS' COMPENSATION CASES

THE PROBLEM

In recent years a new loss phenomenon has arisen within many large corporations. Just as old-fashioned theft rings used to plague many companies and cause staggering losses, this new phenomenon of fraud and malingering in workers' compensation cases is costing every bit as much and even has the potential to rise to the top as the number one loss factor in many companies today. As the security industry has come of age and gone steadily toward professionalization, many dishonest employees have found other ways to supplement their income.

Unlike internal theft, where there is a risk of being fired and even prosecuted, dishonest employees have found that there is little or no risk in the area of misusing workers' compensation and that they have no one in authority, such as a corporate security department, to contend with. By the same token, the attitude of many line executives within companies is that workers' compensation is "somebody else's problem." The "somebody" to whom they refer is usually the insurance company or perhaps the corporate insurance department.

In corporations that are not self-insured in workers' comp and who look to carriers to provide service in this area, it is not unusual to find millions of dollars of the company's money tied up in so-called reserves held by the insurance carrier. It is rare indeed for any large corporation to carry 100 percent pure workers' compensation insurance because of the tremendous costs involved. Rather, companies generally have a very high deductible, or what is referred to as a stop-loss, that can be anywhere from $100,000 to $200,000 per case. When a workers' compensation case occurs, the first $100,000 or perhaps $200,000 of coverage is the company's own money and the insurance company simply acts as an umbrella coverer for anything in excess of that. This is a tremendous financial burden on the company. A young person within the work force who is injured on the job could easily have a payoff, over his lifetime, of $100,000 or more, depending on age and statutory benefits. It does not take long for a number of these total disability cases to add up to figures exceeding the million-dollar mark. For these and other reasons, many companies have increasingly turned to self-insurance so that they have the use of their own money rather than having the cash tied up in reserves held by the insurance carrier. Either way, the astute security director can immediately see where his department can make a significant financial contribution to the well-being of the company and, in fact, might even be able to justify his entire budget on workers' compensation savings alone.

There is little doubt that, as a result of the improvement in the economy, we have entered a more permissive era. The incentive for fraud has reached significant proportions. Employees read that their company is making substantial profits and know that there is no threat of employee cutbacks. Since the company needs them, if they are injured there is no hurry to return to work because their jobs will be there even after a prolonged absence. They may also sense a renewed permissiveness on the part of their employers, who may have become lax as profits increased.

As a result, insureds and their insurers can see sharp increases in workers' compensation fraud cases. Awareness in this area typically lags behind the deed. When a company develops a reputation for being "soft" on this type of case, it can experience substantial losses. Those companies that are self-insured or have high loss limits will feel these losses directly on their bottom line statements. If danger signs are present, such as a growing number of long-term disability cases, ever-increasing premiums, or deteriorating loss ratios, investigative help might be in order. Long-term disability cases have a one-in-four chance of being fraud, or of being shot through with malingering.

(For clarification, we will distinguish here between fraud and malingering. Fraud cases are cases that commence with no injury and start out with the sole intent of defrauding the company. Malingering, on the other hand, usually involves a bona fide injury but the person eventually recovers. However, they have little or no contact with the company and begin to realize that the disability checks will keep coming as long as they do not return to work.)

ONE COMPANY'S EXPERIENCE

In 1981, Cluett, Peabody & Co., Inc., a major apparel manufacturer, studied the feasibility of self-insuring workers' compensation coverage. The study revealed that there were many old total disability cases still being carried with high reserves by the insurer. With a $100,000 retention per claim, Cluett was anxious to minimize the growing financial burden of these claims.

Like many large corporations, Cluett maintained an internal corporate security department that was primarily engaged in investigation and internal crime prevention efforts. In 1981, as part of a pilot program, the company budgeted $40,000 to investigate suspected fraudulent long-term disability cases. Only one case was successfully resolved that year, for a favorable retro adjustment of $50,000. The rest of the work done in 1981 resulted in savings of $49,000 in 1982. Work done in 1982 paid off in 1983 for just under a half-million dollars. After 1983, the company was completely self-insured, so that reserves were not being set up for the cases. However, payments to claimants still had to be made, and it was possible to track, using independent claims evaluators, what any one particular claim was worth or would have been reserved for by an insurance carrier. The security department simply continued to investigate those cases suspected of involving fraud or malingering.

As a result of this work, the corporation came to certain conclusions, as follows:

1. As stated above, it was found that one out of every four long-term disability cases was either fraudulent or shot through with malingering.
2. Regular communication with the claimant by the local personnel office of the corporation was mandatory. People who have bona fide injuries are much more likely to return to work early if they feel that the company is interested in them. They are also less likely to seek the services of an attorney for purposes of filing a major compensation claim.
3. An outreach program by a medical representative of the corporation is also highly desirable. Not only does this add to the communication with the personnel department, but it can also serve as a trigger for the corporate security department to become involved. This outreach program includes initial claim review by a trained medical representative and may raise a red flag regarding the very nature of the suspected injury or the circumstances under which the injury occurred—for example, the review may find that no one witnessed or heard the injury as it

actually took place. The medical history given to initial interviewers is also included in the medical outreach program.
4.   Monitoring of existing claims may raise a red flag. This can come
about because the claimant does not keep medical or rehabilitation appointments and spot checks by a medical representative
reveal an activity pattern on the part of the claimant inconsistent
with the alleged disability.

Any of the above can act as a trigger for the involvement of the
corporate security department.

Whether the security department itself becomes involved in the
investigation of these claims or farms the work out to a qualified
agency, the most important factor will be the selection of the investigators to do the work. The security director must be absolutely sure
that persons who will handle surveillance on these cases are thoroughly competent in the art of surveillance.

Not only do the investigators have to be expert in the art of
surveillance techniques, they must also be resourceful in getting the
claimant involved in physical activity without engaging in entrapment. They also have to be skilled in conventional investigative
techniques, because some facets of these cases require investigation
comparable to handling a background check. This is especially true
where evidence is being developed of prior workers' compensation
cases in former places of employment. Perhaps the claimant is even
currently employed while still receiving disability checks.

Self-insured companies can join a self-insurers' association that
maintains regional index bureaus that can be researched for prior
claims. There are also a number of data banks available in various
states for the investigator to check to determine whether past awards
were made on prior claims.

Finally, the investigator must know the medical aspects of the
case. If surveillance is called for, he or she must know precisely what
types of physical activity are precluded by the claimed injury.

As already noted, the primary consideration is that the privacy
of the claimant not be invaded. For this reason, surveillance vans
are particularly useful. The investigator should always advise local
police that he or she will be in a particular neighborhood. This
forestalls interference if a neighbor reports a suspicious vehicle parked
for an apparently undue period of time in a given spot. If the surveillance requires considerable time, the investigator can even live
in the vehicle for several days. Using a periscope and telephoto
lenses, he or she can observe subjects as they come out of their homes
(see Figure 6.1). Radio communication can be maintained with a
back-up vehicle that can be used to "tail" in case the subject leaves
home.

Catching subjects in a public place, such as a nearby softball field, a building materials yard, or their own front yard, is a problem that patience can solve. In the prolonged time period typical of fraudulent or malingering cases, subjects often grow careless, and only the most obvious surveillance will arouse their suspicions.

Following are excerpts from reports of typical claims that have been investigated:

Wilmington, DE, Exposure: $35,000, Injury: Lumbar Strain. "This individual was observed at her residence several weekends in a row. She alleged she was totally disabled, unable to lift, to bend, or to turn her head to drive a car.

"She was filmed moving plants and heavy picnic hampers from one vehicle to another and from her residence to a vehicle. This procedure took approximately 30 to 45 minutes every time that it was observed. She sustained this activity over a period of time without the use of any braces or aids, walking without a limp and able to lift, bend, and carry several bulky items at a time. After she had her car completely loaded, she would meet her husband and they would go to the beach. There they had a boat that they were refurbishing. She sanded the hull of the boat, showing no sign of disability or strain to her back.

"At one point, she picked up the large family dog and placed it in the vehicle before they left for the beach. The same continued activities were repeated over and over. The claimant never stopped to rest."

Atlanta, GA, Exposure: $35,000, Injury: Lumbar Strain—Total Disability. "Investigation revealed claimant used her disability checks to finance a would-be modeling career. She spent most of her time going to modeling auditions.

"In this case, the claimant was advised that (fake) auditions were being held for models who have the opportunity to pose for pictures and movies for a client attempting to sell sports equipment. Several models were on hand as props and this particular claimant, when she arrived with her husband, was put through the paces of doing several strenuous activities. She was filmed climbing monkey bars utilizing her arms and her legs. She proceeded to jump rope, a rather strenuous activity for someone who claimed to have been totally disabled by a back injury. She was asked to turn and move in several different positions showing that she had mobility in her back and legs. She then did straight-leg sit ups on a lounge chair. This was done for several minutes, and she appeared to be having a good time. She proceeded to ride a stationary bicycle. Prior to this activity, the tension on the bicycle was turned as tight as possible, creating as much difficulty as possible in peddling the bicycle. She did this relatively easily without a sign of a strain or disability. This particular activity continued for approximately six minutes. Several angles of this were filmed to give the doctors and potential court hearing officers the opportunity to observe the claimant from various angles.

"She was asked to dive and swim in the swimming pool at this location to show that she had use of her arms and legs and was able to sustain this activity for several minutes. She was able to bend at the knees, arch her back and dive into the pool without any difficulty whatsoever. This claimant was found to have been using her workers' compensation payments to further a potential modeling career. She bragged to her fellow workers of this."

The claimant in the role of prospective model was not being enticed into doing anything that she would not ordinarily do as a regular part of many auditions. In addition, it was a semi-public situation. This precluded the defense of entrapment.

New York, NY, Exposure: $150,000, Injury: Lumbar Strain. "The claimant alleged to have fallen on the job and hurt her back and neck and stated that she was totally disabled and unable to take care of herself, drive a car, ride in a car for prolonged periods, carry anything whatsoever in her arms, bend her arms, or stoop. This claimant was intercepted in Atlanta and followed to New Orleans after driving 1200 miles. The claimant was filmed leaving her motel and repacking the vehicle for her departure to Florida. The claimant drove for four-hour intervals at which time she would stop for gas and then continue on her trip. She was accompanied by a relative who did a minor part of the driving. She had no problem carrying several bundles down three flights of steps unaided without any sign of a disability. She was carrying a cane over her left arm. She did the major loading of the large automobile, a sustained activity. She was filmed bending at the waist several times, stretching into the trunk compartment of the vehicle. Repeatedly she bent, fully extending herself to pick up a heavy box and place it in the trunk of the vehicle. She did this without any sign of a disability. She then picked up her cane and placed it in the trunk of the vehicle. She never once used the cane on the entire trip. She moved without any sign of a limp."

As these cases illustrate, the investigator should vary methods, always remaining within legal and ethical perimeters. The case should be built using visual evidence that graphically shows fraud or malingering and is impossible for any fair-minded authority to ignore.

MAKING USE OF THE EVIDENCE GATHERED

Once the evidence is gathered, it must be decided how to use the information. Unlike criminal cases, where the security director will probably make these decisions in conjunction with the police and prosecutor, fraud and malingering cases are usually handled by the company's medical representatives, insurance departments, or the attorneys who have been retained to defend the company in this type of case. The security director should be content simply to turn over the evidence obtained and be prepared to gather more evidence if those making the decisions indicate that additional evidence is needed.

Oftentimes, photographic evidence can be shown to a doctor who is considered to be honest and fair in his treatment of these cases. Many times, people will obtain a doctor's certification to remain out of work and will successfully deceive the doctor about the true nature of the injuries. It has been the author's experience that many physicians, once they have viewed surveillance films that show physical activity contradictory to the injury claim, will immediately withdraw certification that the person is disabled. This of course forces the employee to return to work and eliminates the possibility of a long-term claim.

In other cases, the claimant may already have retained the services of an attorney and filed suit under the Worker's Compensation Act for long-term disability. In these cases, the lawyer retained by the company or the claim's handling agency becomes the "quarterback" of the investigative team. It is he or she who must decide whether the evidence is sufficient or if additional evidence is needed. Many times, claimants will testify that the photographic evidence caught them on a "good day" but that then they were totally bedridden for the next several days because of an excess of physical activity. For this reason, it is usually necessary to successfully obtain photographic evidence on succeeding days in order to show a pattern of routine physical activity.

In summary, it is clear that the security director is in a position to make significant contributions to the bottom line of the company by taking on the additional activity of investigating workers' compensation claims.

As in the budget-making process, many assumptions have to be made when it comes to loss prevention and justifying the security department. In the area of workers' compensation claims, however, it is quite easy for the director to show actual figures of savings or even recovery to the corporation by his efforts, rather than having to rely on assumptions for budgeting purposes. In any large corporation, it is almost a given that these large sums of money are there for the security director to find—and should *go for it!*

Appendixes

Appendix 1
Security Inspection Report

Date of original inspection _____
Date of last inspection _____
Date of this inspection _____

COMPLETE IN QUADRUPLICATE:
  ORIGINAL—Plant Manager
  DUPLICATE—
  TRIPLICATE—Corp. Security
  QUADRUPLICATE—Regional Security
Officials interviewed during survey

Name & Address
of Location

_____

_____

_____

_____

_____   _____
        (Names)   **(Titles)**

Instructions: All "NO" answers to be explained on separate page. Also, all descriptions called for and any question where improved control is needed.

Petty Cash Count:
  Cash authorized _____
  Cash on hand _____
  Receipts & Vouchers _____
  Over/Short _____
Volume in last fiscal year _____

$ Overage or	Raw Materials _____
(Loss) in last	In Process _____
fiscal year	Finished Stock _____

Total Number of Personnel (everyone headquartered in building)

Warehse	Factory	Drivers	Off.	Salrd Supvrs. & Exec.

Type of Building (describe fully)

                        Y N

PERSONNEL

1. Is the application form completed properly and signed?

2. Where a security screening program is in effect, have polygraph tests or Reid Reports been administered to all applications for sensitive positions?

Y N

PERSONNEL (cont'd)

3. Are references of applicants for sensitive positions checked by either letter or telephone?

4. Are completed reference letters or telephone checklists placed in the personal folder?

5. Are criminal activity checks made of applicants for sensitive positions?

7. Are there any company rules which have been put in writing?

8. Are they adequate for this location?

9. Are company rules posted?

10. Are disciplinary actions reduced to writing and placed in personnel files?

11. Are regular safety-security meetings held?
    Did you review the minutes of the last three meetings?

12. Is the Incident Report Form regularly in use?

13. Is the Monthly Security Inspection Report in use?
    Date of last report:

14. Has responsibility for overall security been delegated to one employee?
    Name:

GUARDS & WATCHMEN

21. Are guards or watchmen utilized at this location? Attach post No's and hours of coverage if any change since last report.

22. Is coverage adequate for this location?

24. Describe current rate of pay for guards and watchmen.

25. If agency guards what do we pay agency? _____
    What do the men receive?

27. Is there a guard manual of written rules and regulations for the night watchmen and guard force?

28. Are present instructions, rules and regulations adequate for current conditions?
    (Attach any changes in guard manual since last report)

30. Is a daily log maintained giving full particulars of all persons entering and leaving the building, except at starting and quitting time?

31. Is the Guard's Daily Report in use?
    Who receives the report, and takes follow-up action?

    How long retained? _____

33. List type of firearms and other equipment carried by guards.
    Is equipment owned by Company Guard Agency or personal property of guards?

36. Is instruction and training given to guards and watchmen in the use of firearms and emergency equipment?
    By whom? _____

KEYS, ALARM AND WATCHCLOCK SYSTEMS

41. List key holders by name, position, locks or doors, type of key.
    Number of master keys? _____
    Where and how are spares secured _____
    Normal opening and closing times of office door if not on alarm?

42. Are keys withheld from alarm company? If not is key sealed?

43. Are locks changed when a key is lost?

Y N

44. Are locks changed when a key holder leaves the company?
Date locks were last changed:

45. Are guard's building keys and gate keys maintained in secure place when not actually in use?

46. Are the buildings equipped with burglar or other type alarms? If so, describe type of alarms, i.e., central station and name of company, local alarm to police, F.D., outside bell, internal day alarms, etc.

47. List burglar alarm circuit No. area covered, title of card holders and normal opening and closing times by days.

48. Was a review of alarm company or time recorder lock reports of unusual openings and closings since last inspection found to be negative?

49. Are all alarm systems tested regularly? Did you personally make a test of all perimeter alarms?
Types of system tested? _____

50. Describe any changes since last report in floor-plan showing the following:
a) Entrances and exits (including overhead doors).
b) Exits connected with alarms and/or padlocked.
c) Watchman's clock stations, numbered in sequence.
d) Guard stations.
e) Fire stations.

51. Did you make a clock round with the guard?
Is the number of stations and location adequate?
Describe frequency of rounds, type system used, if central station controlled, etc.

52. How often are watch clock tapes or discs examined?
_____
By whom?_____
Are tapes or discs retained until they are examined by insurance inspectors and Corporate security officers?

TRANSPORTATION SECURITY
54. Are adequate security procedures taken when merchandise is left in trailers or box cars?

55. Is responsible person present on docks at all times when receiving and shipping doors are open?
Title:

56. Are shipping and receiving rooms properly separated?

57. At warehouse locations, are shipping activities, which are performed during other than normal working hours, subject to extra security measure?
Explain:

58. Are truck driver movements restricted from the stock areas?
(Describe amount of access).

59. Is a well defined and carefully executed plan in effect for the use of security seals on Company or leased trucks which are used to transfer products or finished goods between inter-companies, plants and warehouses? Describe plan, name person in charge of supervision of plan and method used for custody of seals.

60. If seals are not used, have paper controls been set up?
(If so, describe fully).

Y N

INTERNAL CONTROLS

61. Is a permanent access or pass system in effect for off hours?
    Covers: (List by name and title)

62. Is employee identification adequate?

63. Is procedure for handling returns and/or seconds adequate for security purposes?

64. Does procedure for disposal of waste cartons, trash, etc. minimize opportunity for theft?
    Did you inspect the trash?
    (Describe controls set up)

65. If there are restricted areas, buildings, or offices on the premises, are these areas protected? (Describe)

66. Are janitors, maintenance men, and clean up crews properly supervised for control of theft activity?
    (Describe)

67. Are employees required to enter and leave the building only via the _____ door?

68. Are employees prohibited from taking lunch boxes, packages, purses or handbags, etc., into stock and working areas?

69. Are employees' packages which are brought into the building, stored in their lockers or other place approved by management?

70. Are the locker space and restrooms outside stock and working areas?

72. Is there local physical inspection of handbags, packages, lunch boxes, etc., made as employees leave the building?
    Is the inspection complete as opposed to a spot check?
    Did you personally observe or make an inspection?
    Who makes the inspection?

    Where is the inspection performed? _____
    How often is the inspection performed? _____

74. Are employees prohibited from remaining in stock and working areas during lunch periods?

75. Is a supervisor on duty during lunch periods?

76. Is procedure for pick-up of employee purchases in conformity with good security?
    (Describe fully)

78. Are employees' cars parked only in areas a secure distance from shipping and receiving doors?

80. Did you make an inspection of lockers, work stations, sensitive areas, etc.?
    List names of questionable products, location and name of employee.

81. Are lavatories and refuse containers free of improper items?

82. Are all cases in the full case area full and unopened?

PERIMETER SECURITY

106. Did the perimeter security check reveal that proper security measures are in use? (Outside of buildings, ground floor, basement windows, flood-lights, skylights, doors, approach to roof, etc.)

Y N

PERIMETER SECURITY (cont'd)

107. Did you walk the fence line?
Is the present condition of fence perimeter adequate? List any holes, breaks, etc.
Describe height, type and material of fence.

_____

108. When fence gates are not in use, are they kept closed?

109. When gates are not guarded, are they securely locked?

MISCELLANEOUS
115. List any security deficiencies remaining since last inspection.

116. List any personal observations during this Security Inspection that indicate laxness in administration of security, gambling, drinking, leaving work place, sleeping on job, etc.

117. Describe any unusual political or labor practices that could have some bearing on security.

118. On Security Department copies only, show date of your last personal contact with local police sources.

Submitted by: _____

Appendix 2
Security Inspection Report

Retail Stores Division

Distribution: (_____ copies)
Orig:
Dup:
Trip:
Quad:

Company: _____
Store Location: _____
Date: _____ Prepared by _____
Sales: _____ % Shrink _____ For Period_____

Officials interviewed _____
during survey: _____
                (Names)   (Titles)

Instructions: All "NO" answers are to be explained on separate page; include all descriptions required; note where improved control is needed. SN denotes See Notes; NA denotes Not Applicable at this location.

Description of building: (Sq. ft. _____)
_____
_____

Number of employees in the building

	Exec	Office	Sales	Ship/Rec.	Alter	Wrap	Porters	Leased
Full Time								
Part Time								

        Y N

1. PERSONNEL
Does inspection of randomly selected personnel files verify that:

a. The application form is properly completed?

b. Adequate references have been checked?

c. Where a security screening program is in effect, have polygraph tests or Reid reports been administered to all persons having access to money and/or merchandise?

d. Fair credit notification, Policy acceptance, and Salary withholding agreements are signed?

Y N

PERSONNEL (cont'd)

e. Serious infractions of Company rules are documented in writing by use of an employee consultation or disciplinary action form?

2. PHYSICAL SECURITY-ALARMS (external)
This building is protected by (   ) circuits which transmit alarms to:

a. Co.: _____

City: _____ Phone: _____

Cir# _____ covers _____

_____

Cir# _____ covers _____

_____

Cir# _____ covers _____

_____

b. Card Holders for:

Cir# _____ are:

                     Name   Title

_____

_____

_____

_____

Cir# _____ are _____

_____

_____

c. Cir#_____was tested and it transmitted an alarm as required. It took _____ minutes for (phone) (physical) response.

Cir#_____was tested and it transmitted an alarm as required. It took _____ minutes for (phone) (physical) response.

d. Operations should receive reports of *unusual* openings and closings. Did your review of the latter fail to reveal any pattern?

e. Have adequate security provisions been made for personnel required to come in early or stay late?

f. Describe any changes since last report in floor-plan showing the following:
    Entrance and exits, incl. overhead doors
    Exits connected with alarm.

3. PHYSICAL SECURITY—ALARMS (internal)

a. Do all non-public exit doors have audible panic type alarms?

b. Was each tested and found to be in working order?

c. Was sound level sufficient to alert management?

PHYSICAL SECURITY—ALARMS (cont'd)

d. By-pass keys are possessed by:

Name	Title

4. PHYSICAL SECURITY—LOCKS

Locks must be changed when an identifiable key is lost or a key holder leaves the company. Padlocks should be kept in locked position.

a. Peripheral door keys are possessed by:

Name	Title

b. Were locks changed:
When the last key-holder left the company? _____
Whenever an identifiable key is lost? _____

Date locks were last changed _____

c. Detail lock repairs indicated:

5. DISASTER/THREATS EMERGENCIES

a. Has an organization for handling emergencies been established? _____

b. Are instructions adequate for this location? _____

c. Are supervisory personnel familiar with these instructions? _____

d. Does switchboard operator have appropriate instruction sheet and acknowledge understanding? _____

e. Date of last Fire Drill? _____

f. List any unreported incidents since last inspection:

6. EMPLOYEE CONTROL—ENTRANCE AND OWN/GOODS

Employees should be prohibited from taking own goods such as lunches, packages, outerwear and other personal belongings into stock, office and selling areas.

a. Is store free of above violations? _____

b. Are employees' cars parked only in areas a secure distance from shipping and receiving doors?

EMPLOYEE CONTROL—ENTRANCE AND OWN/GOODS (cont'd)

c. Are employees required to enter and leave the building only via the _____ door?
   This should include lunch and rest periods.

d. Are employee lockers provided?

e. If so, is the location appropriate for their intended purpose?

f. Are lockers inspected?
   By whom:
   Frequency: Last time:

g. Where lockers are not provided, describe alternative security provisions for personal belongings.

h. Is there a physical inspection of packages, lunch boxes, and personal belongings, etc., made as employees leave the building?

i. Is the inspection complete as opposed to a spot check?

j. Who makes the inspection:

k. Where is the inspection performed?

l. How often made:

7. EMPLOYEE CONTROL—PURCHASES

a. Is procedure for employee purchases in conformity with good security?

b. Is a central holding area provided and use enforced?

c. What are the provisions to deter unauthorized discounts to friends and/or relatives:

8. OFFICE

a. Is the requirement to exclude unauthorized personnel enforced?

b. Is reserve stock of: cash refund; charge credit; merchandise due bills; own goods sales checks; and gift bonds adequately secured?

c. Safe combination holders are:
   Name   Title

d. Date last changed:
   Reason:

e. If alarmed, type

f. Is change drawer locked when not in use?

9. OPERATING FUND

a. Did inspection fail to reveal any merchandise or money IOU's or post-dated personal checks in the operating fund?

Y N

OPERATING FUND (cont'd)

b. The daily cash report (dated)_____ listing $_____ corresponds with validated bank deposit receipt (dated) _____ for $_____

c. Describe the security provided for transporting money to bank.
_____
_____
_____

d. Is manager provided with timely record of cash overages and shortages for each person or Register?

10. **SALES RECORDING AND CASHIERING**

a. Are you satisfied based on personal observation that sales personnel are adhering to established company sales recording policy?

b. Does this include the requirement that all sales are recorded prior to customer departure?

c. Does sales personnel compare signatures on all charged purchases with charge card or other I.D.?

d. Did your observation indicate an adherence to the requirement that all over-rings/void slips receive supervisor's signature at the time of occurrence?

e. Does night closing procedure include stripping cash registers of money, leaving drawers ajar, and an accounting for monies turned in?

f. Does the daily cash report list each register observed on the premises?

11. **REFUNDS**—Management should physically inspect all returned goods and affix his signature in front of customer.

a. Is refund procedure for this location adequate? If not, recommend accordingly. _____
_____
_____
_____
_____

b. Is sales ticket and/or cash register receipt defaced when credit voucher or refund is issued?

12. **SHIPPING/RECEIVING**

a. Did your inspection of packages prepared for delivery (UPS, Parcel Post, etc.) contain only authorized and cash register validated labels?

b. Where supplemental labels are required, are controls adequate to preclude unauthorized usage?

c. Did your inspection of transfer procedures reveal adherence to established policy?

d. Did spot check counts reveal discrepancies?

e. Are transfer hangers, cages, and tanks sealable?

f. Is there a well-defined and carefully executed plan in effect for the use of security seals on both transfer containers and company trucks?

(NOTE: Management should be reminded to inspect seals for tampering prior to removal.)

g. Is the manifest prepared neatly, correctly and completely with attention to form and seal numbers?

SHIPPING/RECEIVING (cont'd)

    h. A representative of management should be present on the dock at all times when receiving doors are open. Except for truck loading/unloading, drivers should not be permitted in the receiving area. Are you satisfied these requirements are being met?

    i. When unresolved discrepancies in counts exist, is the policy to notify security consistently followed?

13. WASTE DISPOSAL

    a. Does procedure for disposal of waste cartons, trash, etc., minimize opportunities for theft?

    b. Are boxes crushed at the department level?

    c. Does management periodically inspect trash?

    d. Does management personally supervise its removal outside?

    e. Results of your trash inspection:

14. DAMAGED MERCHANDISE

    a. Are existing procedures adequate to insure expeditious processing of damaged merchandise to minimize losses?

    b. Are controls sufficient to prevent employees from taking damaged merchandise for personal use?

15. SALES SUPPORTING AREAS

    a. Fitting Rooms:

       (1) Are unused rooms or banks effectively closed off?

       (2) Describe any evidence of shoplifting:

       (3) If improved controls are needed, describe:

    b. Alteration Work Rooms:
       Do all garments in the alteration department have an alteration tag plus sales check, own goods ticket or repair memo? List all discrepancies.

    c. Display:
       (1) Is the requirement to sign in and out major garments for display being enforced?

       (2) Is all merchandise found in the display room properly documented?

    d. Advertising:
       Is the requirement to sign in and out major garments for advertising being enforced?

SALES SUPPORTING AREAS (cont'd)

e. Forward Stock Rooms:
Holds—is tagging policy being followed which requires proper authorization, 3-day maximum and expeditious return to stock if not purchased?

16. SECURITY FILE
To insure compliance with corporate standards and minimize the opportunity for adverse litigation, each store should have a security file. Did your inspection of this file confirm that:
a. It contains a copy of the security manual?

b. The manager is completing his monthly Security Inspection Check List?

c. Incident Report Forms are being completed for each required occasion?

d. There were no unreported instances of suspected or actual dishonesty or known losses?

e. A supply of apprehension support forms are available?
These should include blank "confession" and "general releases."

f. It contains a list of emergency telephone numbers, including local police, fire and ambulance.

17. SHOPLIFTING
a. Are cash registers/check-out areas designed in a manner to preclude customer accessibility to cash drawers, bags, boxes and sales recording media?

b. Is valuable merchandise displayed with security in mind? If not, recommend accordingly?

c. Is arrangement of displays such as to preclude obstructed views?

d. If the security implications of this location suggest a need for the sealing of all customer packages, demonstrate to management how this can be accomplished in good taste by use of string handles taped to package.

e. What are the elements needed for a valid shoplifting apprehension at this location?

f. Have all members of Management been briefed in proper apprehension procedures and aware of the foregoing required elements?

g. Are you satisfied that there is a continuous educational effort directed at making employees aware of this problem?

h. Are new employees thoroughly familiar with the reward program?

i. Did they receive a personal copy of the reward brochure and anti-shoplifting pamphlet?

j. List other training aides being used:

Y N

SHOPLIFTING (cont'd)

k. If appropriate, recommend anti-shoplifting devices such as hanger guards, plastic ties, alternating hangers, observation ports, etc.

_____
_____
_____
_____

l. Is the anti-shoplifting coverage for this store adequate?

18. GENERAL
a. Are *Security Rules and Regulations* displayed prominently in this store?

b. Specific management request for additional security:

_____
_____

c. List any personal observations made during this security inspection that indicate laxness in administration of security, i.e., gambling, drinking, leaving work place, sleeping on job.

_____
_____
_____
_____
_____

d. Is the store climate such to create proper spirit of discipline and alertness to the security problem?

e. What security problems discovered during previous visit still exist? _____

_____
_____
_____

f. Describe any unusual political or labor practices which might have a bearing on security: _____

_____
_____
_____
_____

g. Local Police Department _____
                                    (Phone)
_____
(P. Larc. = _____) (G. Larc. = _____)

Age considered adult _____
(On security department copies only, show local police contacts and appropriate comments, if any)

_____
_____
_____
_____

NOTE:
The remaining portion of this Inspection Report pertains to Safety and compliance with the OSHA Act. When possible, deficiencies should be corrected "on-the-spot." If unable to do so, management must be advised of those deficiencies during your "Post Inspection" discussion with management.

19. HOUSEKEEPING & MAINTENANCE
a. Are all floors and stairways free of obstructions and slipping hazards?

b. Are all floor surfaces, carpets, tile, etc., in good condition, sidewalks adjacent to store free of slipping and tripping hazards?

c. Are stairs in good condition, handrails secure and lighting adequate?

d. Are all exit doors easily operated, exit signs and lights in good condition, exits unobstructed?

e. Is all glass, external and internal, including mirrors, free of cracks, chips, etc.?

f. Is all furniture in use in safe condition, solid, free of cracks, splinters, burrs, projections, etc.?

g. Are all ladders and fitting stands in sturdy, tight condition, free of cracks, splinters and defective hardware?

h. Are swing racks in good condition, easily operated?

i. Are utility closets orderly and free of debris?

j. Are toilet facilities bright, clean, ventilated, with adequate supplies?

20. ELECTRICAL SAFETY
a. Are electrical outlets ample so that multiple plugs and extension cords for other than temporary wiring are not used?

b. Are flexible cords in good condition and free of splices?

c. Are electrical cabinets kept closed and clear for 30" in front?

d. Has the electrical system been checked and serviced by a licensed electrician within the past year?

e. Is emergency lighting operative in simulated power failure?

f. Has periodic inspection and service of all elevator equipment been provided?

g. Are escalator emergency shut-off buttons operative; has periodic inspection and service of all escalator equipment been provided?

21. FIRE PROTECTION
a. Are adequate fire extinguishers in place, accessible, ready for use—tags dated and signed—*employees trained in use?*

b. Are sprinkler heads unobstructed?
   (Minimum clearance 18",—36" when storage height exceeds 15'.)

c. Is fire hose in place, unobstructed and ready for use?

d. Are flammable wastes (wrappings, tissues, etc.) stored in covered metal containers and removed from the premises daily or more frequently if necessary?

e. Are flammable liquids, paints, thinners, etc., safely stored and used in a safe manner?

f. When installed is the fire alarm system under the supervision of qualified persons who test it weekly?

   (1) Are all employees instructed in its use,
   (2) Is the fire department telephone number properly posted?

g. Are adequate and strategically placed ash trays provided, floors free of cigarette butts and "No Smoking" signs posted in prohibited areas?

h. Are all automatic and self-closing fire doors operative? Fire doors to stairs kept closed? Moveable parts of fire escapes operable?

FIRE PROTECTION (cont'd)

i. Where remodeling work, painting or decorating is in progress, is an inspection made at the end of each day to safeguard the area?

j. Are pressing irons always "parked" on proper stands and turned off during long idle periods and at the end of the working day?

22. MISCELLANEOUS—SAFETY

a. Do Employees know the procedure in event of an accident to a customer or fellow employee?

b. Are the necessary emergency telephone numbers correct and properly posted—police, fire, medical, security?

c. Are employees knowledgeable in procedures for emergency evacuation of all store occupants?

d. Are all hand tools (scissors, knives, hammers, etc.) in safe condition and properly stored?
Power tools properly guarded?

e. Is First Aid Kit adequate and kept properly filled?

f. Is the OSHA poster conspicuously displayed?

g. Do all electric ventilating fans within reach have a protective shroud with openings small enough to preclude accidental blade injury?

h. Do all sewing machines have spring type needle guards and/or plastic eye shields?

Appendix 3: Forms for On-Going Investigations Permitted Under Section 7(d) of the Employee Polygraph Protection Act of 1988

Form 101
Revised 12/5/88

EMPLOYER'S STATEMENT TO EMPLOYEE
WITH RESPECT TO ONGOING INVESTIGATION AND NOTICE
OF REQUEST FOR POLYGRAPH TEST

Employer's Name: _____
Business Address: _____
                        Street   City   State   Zip

Employee's Name: _____
Address of location
where Employee is employed:
                        _____
                        Street   City   State   Zip

EMPLOYER'S STATEMENT TO EMPLOYEE WITH RESPECT TO ONGOING
INVESTIGATIONS
1. **Incident or activity being investigated.**
   (A) **Description of incident or activity:** _____
   _____
   (B) **Date or time period in which incident or activity is believed to have**
       occurred: _____
   (C) **Location(s) where incident or activity is believed to have taken**
       place: _____
   (D) **Incident or activity involved: [ ] Money   [ ] Merchandise**
       [ ] Other _____
   (E) **Approximate dollar amount, if ascertained:**
       $ _____
2. **Type of economic loss under investigation.**
   [ ] **Theft**   [ ] **Embezzlement**   [ ] **Misappropriation**
   [ ] **Unlawful industrial espionage or sabotage**   [ ] **Check kiting**
   [ ] **Money laundering**   [ ] **Misappropriation of confidential or**
                                       secret information
   [ ] **Other** _____
3. **If incident or activity involved money, merchandise, or other property,**
area in which such money, merchandise, or property is located and Em-
ployee's access thereto:

_____

4. **Basis of Employer's reasonable suspicion that Employee was involved**
in the incident or activity under investigation.
   (A) **Information from a co-worker or other individual:**

_____

(Note: The identity of a co-worker or other individual providing information
used to establish reasonable suspicion need not be revealed.)
   (B) **Employee's behavior, demeanor, or conduct:**

_____
_____

(C) **Inconsistencies between facts, claims, or statements that surfaced during the investigation:**

_____

_____

(D) **Circumstances surrounding access or opportunity, such as its unauthorized or unusual nature:**

_____

_____

(E) **Other basis for reasonable suspicion:**

_____

_____

NOTICE TO EMPLOYEE OF REQUEST FOR POLYGRAPH TEST.

(A) **You are requested to appear for a polygraph test at the offices of John E. Reid and Associates, Inc., 250 S. Wacker Drive, Chicago, Illinois on ___(date)___ at ___(time)___ .**

(B) **You have the right to consult with counsel or an employee representative before each phase of the polygraph test. However, the attorney or employee representative will not be permitted in the room where the examination is administered during the actual testing phase.**

The undersigned, as an authorized representative of the Employer, hereby states as follows:

(A) **The information contained herein is true to the best of my knowledge, information, and belief.**

(B) **There is a reasonable suspicion that the Employee was involved in the incident or activity under investigation.**

(C) **A copy of the above statement was delivered to the Employee named herein on ___(date)___ at ___(time)___ .**

Date: _____   _____
                                        Signature
                                        Please print:
                                        _____
                                        Name
                                        _____
                                        Title or position

Received a copy of the above statement.
Date: _____   _____
                                        Employee
Witnessed by:

_____

_____

NOTE: (1) **This statement must be in a language understood by the Employee.**

(2) **A copy of this statement must be delivered to the Employee at least 48 hours prior to the time of the polygraph test, excluding weekend days and holidays.**

(3) **This statement must be signed by a person (other than a polygraph examiner) authorized to legally bind the Employer and must be retained by the Employer for at least three years.**

Form 102
Revised 12/5/88

EMPLOYER'S NOTICE TO
JOHN E. REID AND ASSOCIATES, INC.
OF
EMPLOYEE TO BE ADMINISTERED A POLYGRAPH EXAMINATION
PURSUANT TO
SECTION 7(d) OF THE EMPLOYEE POLYGRAPH
PROTECTION ACT OF 1988

Employer's Name: _____

Business Address: _____
               Street   **City**   **State**   **Zip**

Employee's Name: _____
Address of location where
Employee is employed:

               Street   **City**   **State**   **Zip**

PLEASE TAKE NOTICE that the above-named employee is to be administered a polygraph examination in connection with an ongoing investigation, pursuant to Section 7(d) of the Employee Polygraph Protection Act of 1988 and the applicable Department of Labor Regulations.

Dated: _____   _____

                                         Signature

                                       Please print:

                                       _____

                                       Name

                                       _____

                                       Title or position

Received a copy of the above notice.
Date: _____   **John E. Reid and Associates, Inc.**
                                       By: _____

Form 103
Revised 12/5/88

POLYGRAPH EXAMINER'S NOTICE TO
EMPLOYEE-EXAMINEE REGARDING TEST

Polygraph Firm: John E. Reid and Associates, Inc.

Business Address: 250 South Wacker Drive
Chicago, Illinois 60606

Name of Examiner: _____

Employee-Examinee's Name: _____
Home Address: _____
               Street   City   State   Zip

Employer's Name: _____
Business Address: _____
               Street   City   State   Zip

1. Date, time, and location of polygraph test.
   (A) Date: _____
   (B) Time: _____
   (C) Location: 250 South Wacker Drive, Chicago, Illinois
2. The Employee-Examinee has the right to obtain and consult with legal counsel or an employee representative before each phase of the test, i.e.: the pretest phase (which is this phase); the actual testing phase; and the post-test phase.
3. The polygraph test is for the purpose of determining the truthfulness of the Employee-Examinee's answers to the following relevant questions, which shall be asked during the actual testing phase:
   (A) _____

   (B) _____

   (C) _____

   (D) _____

4. In addition thereto, the following questions will be asked the Employee-Examinee during the actual testing phase:
   (A) _____

   (B) _____

   (C) _____

   (D) _____

   (E) _____

(F) _____

(G) _____

5. During the polygraph test, there will be:
   (A) a pretest interview in which the polygraph examiner goes over the facts and reviews with the Employee-Examinee the relevant questions to be asked on the test.
   (B) the test itself in which the Employee-Examinee is asked the relevant questions, as well as certain other questions (including those needed for comparison purposes) while his or her physiological responses are being recorded by a polygraph instrument. A minimum of two polygraph charts will be run in which the same relevant questions and other questions will be asked in the same or a different order. Also, a chart may be run during which the Employee-Examinee is asked the number of a card selected by the Employee-Examinee from several cards offered the Employee-Examinee by the polygraph examiner.
   (C) a post-test interview in which the Employee-Examinee is afforded a reasonable opportunity to explain and eliminate any reactions which are evident on the polygraph charts.
6. The polygraph instrument records the following physiological responses:
   (a) breathing or respiration; (b) blood pressure and pulse rate; and (c) electricity passing over the surface of the skin.

The undersigned, a polygraph examiner employed by John E. Reid and Associates, Inc., hereby states as follows:
   (A) The information contained herein is true to the best of his knowledge, information, and belief.
   (B) He is a duly licensed polygraph examiner in the state of Illinois.
   (C) During the pretest phase, he explained or caused to be explained, in a language understood by the Employee-Examinee, the contents of the above and foregoing Polygraph Examiner's Notice to Employee-Examinee Regarding Test and delivered a copy of the above Notice to the Employee-Examinee.
   (D) Also, during the pretest phase, he read or caused to be read in a language understood by the Employee-Examinee, the contents of a Notice to Examinee and delivered a copy of said notice to the Employee-Examinee. Said Notice is in the same form as set forth in Appendix A to the Department of Labor Interim Final Regulations effective December 27, 1988 (published in the Federal Register on October 21, 1988).

Date: _____   _____
                                       Signature

Received a copy of the above Notice.
Date: _____   _____
                                       Examinee

Witnessed by:
_____

_____

Form 104
Revised 12/5/88

NOTICE TO EXAMINEE

Section 8(b) of the Employee Polygraph Protection Act, and Department of Labor regulations (29 CFR 801.22) require that you be given the following information before taking a polygraph examination:

1. (a) The polygraph examination area (does) (does not) contain a two-way mirror, a camera, or other device through which you may be observed.
   (b) Another device, such as those used in conversation or recording, (will) (will not) be used during the examination.
   (c) Both you and the employer have the right, with the other's knowledge, to record electronically the entire examination.
2. (a) You have the right to terminate the test at any time.
   (b) You have the right, and will be given the opportunity, to review all questions to be asked during the test.
   (c) You may not be asked questions in a manner which degrades, or needlessly intrudes.
   (d) You may not be asked any questions concerning: Religious beliefs or opinions; beliefs regarding racial matters; political beliefs or affiliations; matters relating to sexual behavior; beliefs, affiliations, opinions, or lawful activities regarding unions or labor organizations.
   (e) The test may not be conducted if there is sufficient written evidence by a physician that you are suffering from a medical or psychological condition or undergoing treatment that might cause abnormal responses during the examination.
3. (a) The test is not and cannot be required as a condition of employment.
   (b) The employer may not discharge, dismiss, discipline, deny employment or promotion, or otherwise discriminate against you based on the analysis of a polygraph test, or based on your refusal to take such a test without additional evidence which would support such action.
   (c) (1) In connection with an ongoing investigation, the additional evidence required for an employer to take adverse action against you, including termination, may be (A) evidence that you had access to the property that is the subject of the investigation, together with (B) the evidence supporting the employer's reasonable suspicion that you were involved in the incident or activity under investigation.
       (2) Any statement made by you before or during the test may serve as additional supporting evidence for an adverse employment action, as described in 3(b) above, and any admission of criminal conduct by you may be transmitted to an appropriate government law enforcement agency.

4. (a) Information acquired from a polygraph test may be disclosed by the examiner or by the employer only:

      (1) To you or any other person specifically designated in writing by you to receive such information;

      (2) To the employer that requested the test;

      (3) To a court, governmental agency, arbitrator, or mediator that obtains a court order;

      (4) To a U.S. Department of Labor official when specifically designated in writing by you to receive such information.

    (b) Information acquired from a polygraph test may be disclosed by the employer to an appropriate governmental agency without a court order where, and only insofar as, the information disclosed is an admission of criminal conduct.

5. If any of your rights or protections under the law are violated, you have the right to file a complaint with the Wage and Hour Division of the U.S. Department of Labor, or to take action in court against the employer. Employers who violate this law are liable to the affected examinee, who may recover such legal or equitable relief as may be appropriate, including employment, reinstatement, and promotion, payment of lost wages and benefits, and reasonable costs, including attorney's fees. The Secretary of Labor may also bring action to restrain violations of the Act, or may assess civil money penalties against the employer.

6. Your rights under the Act may not be waived, either voluntarily or involuntarily, by contract or otherwise, except as part of a written settlement to a pending action or complaint under the Act, and agreed to and signed by the parties.

I acknowledge that I have received a copy of the above notice, and that it has been read to me.

_____   _____
Signature   Date

(Note: This Notice to Examinee is in the same form as set forth in Appendix A to the Department of Labor's Interim Final Regulations effective December 27, 1988 [published in the Federal Register on October 21, 1988].)

Form 105
Revised 12/5/88

EMPLOYER'S STATEMENT WITH RESPECT TO ADVERSE ACTION FOLLOWING A POLYGRAPH TEST OR THE REFUSAL TO TAKE A POLYGRAPH TEST

Employer's Name: _____

Business Address: _____
                    Street   **City**   **State**   **Zip**

Employee's Name: _____
Address of location where
Employee is employed:
                    Street   **City**   **State**   **Zip**

1. **Date of interview:** _____
2. **Place of interview:** _____
3. **Time period of interview:**
 Beginning: _____
 Ending: _____
4. **Name of Interviewer:** _____
5. **If Employee took a polygraph test:**
 (A) Date polygraph test administered: _____
 (B) Name of polygraph examiner and firm: _____

 (C) Date of polygraph examiner's report: _____
 (D) Opinion or conclusion of polygraph examiner:
 [ ] Truthful   [ ] Deceptive   [ ] Inconclusive
6. **If Employee refused a polygraph test:**
 (A) Date of refusal: _____
 (B) Name of individual to whom refusal was communicated:

7. **Additional supporting evidence to support adverse action:**
 (A) Facts indicating that the Employee had access to the missing or damaged property that is the subject of an ongoing investigation:
 _____
 _____

 (B) Facts leading to the Employer's reasonable suspicion that the Employee was involved in the incident or activity under investigation:
 _____
 _____

 (C) Admissions or statements made by the Employee before, during, or following the polygraph examination:
 _____
 _____

 (D) Other evidence supporting adverse action:
 _____
 _____

8. **Adverse action taken by Employer:**
   [ ] **Discharge effect:** _____
                              date

   [ ] **Suspension effective:** _____ **for period of** _____ **days**
                                 date

   [ ] **Denial of promotion**
   [ ] **Other discipline** _____
                              Please specify

The undersigned, as an authorized representative of the Employer, hereby states as follows:

   (A) The information contained herein is true to the best of my knowledge, information, and belief.

   (B) If the Employee took a polygraph test, a copy of the polygraph examiner's report was delivered to the Employee during the interview. The report contained the polygraph examiner's opinion or conclusion, and each of the relevant questions asked during the polygraph test with the corresponding charted responses. Also, the Employee was interviewed on the basis of the test results.

Date: _____

                              Signature

                              Please print

                              Name

                              Title or position

Note: (1) This Statement should be retained by the Employer for at least three years. A copy need not be delivered to the Employee-Examinee.

        (2) It is unlawful for adverse action to be taken solely on the basis of the polygraph examiner's opinion or conclusion or solely because the Employee-Examinee has refused to take a polygraph test.

        (3) Adverse action may be taken if there is additional evidence supporting the Employee-Examinee's involvement in the incident or activity under investigation.

Form 106
Revised 12-05-88

AGREEMENT BETWEEN
JOHN E. REID AND ASSOCIATES, INC.
AND CLIENT REGARDING POLYGRAPH TESTS
ADMINISTERED UNDER SECTION 7(d) OF THE
EMPLOYEE POLYGRAPH PROTECTION ACT OF 1988

Agreement entered into on _____, 19____, between John E.
Reid and Associates, Inc., an Illinois corporation, 250 Wacker Drive, Chicago, Illinois 60606 (Reid), and

_____,   _____
        (Name)   **(Address)**

_____,   _____
        (City)   **(State)**   **(Zip)**

(Client).
    WITNESSETH:
    WHEREAS, the Employee Polygraph Protection Act of 1988 became effective December 27, 1988 and applies to all employers engaged in interstate commerce with certain exceptions and exemptions set forth therein; and
    WHEREAS, Client desires to continue utilizing polygraph examinations after the effective date of the Act for ongoing investigations under the limited exemption provided for in Section 7(d) of the Act and the Department of Labor's Final Interim Regulations effective December 27, 1988 (published in the Federal Register on October 21, 1988); and
    WHEREAS, Reid is willing to continue administering polygraph examinations for ongoing investigations under the terms and conditions set forth herein.
    NOW, THEREFORE, the parties hereto agree as follows:
    1. Reid and Client acknowledge that they have carefully reviewed the Act and, in particular, the provisions relating to the limited exemption for ongoing investigations under Section 7(d) and said Department of Labor Final Interim Regulations relating thereto.
    2. Reid agrees to fully comply with the provisions of the Act and Regulations in administering polygraph examinations and reporting the opinion or conclusion of the polygraph examiner.
    3. Client agrees to fully comply with the provisions of the Act and Regulations (a) prior to requesting any employee to take a polygraph examination and (b) following the administration of the polygraph examination.
    4. Reid has furnished Client with certain forms which it believes, in good faith, conform with the requirements of Section 7(d) of the Act and the Regulations relating thereto. However, Client acknowledges that it is currently unknown as to how the Department of Labor and the courts will eventually interpret the Act and Regulations; that such forms are considered as guidelines to assist Client in complying with the Act and Regulations; and that Reid is disclaiming any liability in connection therewith.

5. Client agrees to pay Reid for its services in administering polygraph examinations in the amount agreed upon by the parties from time to time, whether it be based upon a per-hour rate or per-test rate. All payments shall be made within ten (10) days of the receipt of Reid's statement, unless otherwise agreed to in writing.

6. The term of this Agreement shall continue until terminated by either party's giving the other party a written notice at least ten (10) days prior to the effective date of termination.

7. This Agreement shall be governed by the laws of the State of Illinois and shall be construed in accordance therewith.

8. Notices hereunder shall be valid and effective for the purposes hereof if delivered in person or mailed by certified or registered mail, return receipt requested, to the respective parties at their addresses herein set forth, or at such other addresses as they may hereafter direct in writing.

Appendix 4: Common Questions About the Employee Polygraph Protection Act

Does the Act prohibit "pen and pencil" tests designed to test a prospective employee's honesty?

No. The Act only restricts the use of polygraphs, deceptographs, voice stress analyzers, psychological stress evaluators, and other similar devices (whether mechanical or electrical) that are used—or the results of which are used—for the purpose of rendering diagnostic opinions on a person's honesty. Neither the Act nor the regulations restrict the use of pen and pencil "honesty" tests or written psychological profile tests.

When interviewing job applicants, is it permissible to consult or inquire about the results of polygraph tests that were performed before the effective date of the Employee Polygraph Protection Act?

No. Under the Act, employers are forbidden from consulting or inquiring about polygraph test results in pre-employment screening— even if the tests were legal when they were performed. So, for example, although it would be perfectly legal for an employer to insist that a job applicant take a polygraph test on December 26, 1988— before the Act's effective date—it would be a violation of the Act for the employer to consult those same test results on December 28, 1988—after the Act went into effect. Except for the limited exemption accorded to the security and drug industries, polygraph test results may not be considered by private sector employers in pre-employment screening. Period.

Does the Act allow employers to polygraph current employees before they are transferred to sensitive positions of trust?

No. The Act only allows employers to polygraph employees in the course of ongoing investigations of economic injury to the employer. Routine or periodic examinations are forbidden by the Act. (Special rules may apply to employees of security firms and to workers in the drug industry who are transferred from non-covered positions to covered positions.)

Reprinted with the permission of the Chamber of Commerce of the United States from *The Employee Polygraph Protection Act: A Guide to Compliance* © 1989.

What does the Act mean when it says that an employee must be shown to have had "access" to the property that is the subject of the investigation?

Before an employee may be polygraphed, it is necessary to show evidence that the employee had "access" to the property or activity that is the subject of the investigation. The legislative history and the regulations make clear that it is not necessary to show that an employee had direct or physical contact with the property at issue. For example, as the regulations note, all employees with authority to enter a warehouse storage area have "access" to the storage area. Moreover, an employee may be held to have "access" to given property by virtue of having access to the means for affecting disposition of the property. Under this example, a bookkeeper with access to inventory records would be held to have access to the property registered in the inventory records.

What does the Act mean when it says that an employer must have "reasonable suspicion" of an employee's involvement in an economic loss?

Besides evidence of "access," before polygraphing an employee, an employer must be able to point to an "observable, articulable basis in fact" which indicates that the employee was involved in, or responsible for, an economic loss. This "reasonable suspicion" must therefore be something more than a mere "hunch." Access or opportunity, standing alone, would not be sufficient to demonstrate "reasonable suspicion." However, the totality of circumstances surrounding the employee's access (such as its unauthorized or unusual nature) could be used to demonstrate a "reasonable suspicion" of an employee's complicity in the loss under investigation, as could evidence bearing on the employee's demeanor or conduct, or inconsistencies between facts discovered or statements made during the course of an investigation.

Before an employee is polygraphed, is it sufficient to provide the employee with a written copy of the employee's rights under the Act?

No. The notice attached (or a similar notice) must also be read aloud to and signed by the employee. Note also that the employee must be provided with an oral, as well as a written description of the polygraph instrument and examination. If the employee cannot understand the English language, these notices must be provided in a language understood by the employee.

Should the examination be tape-recorded?

The Act and regulations give both the employer and the employee the right to tape-record the full examination, whether by audiotape or videotape, so long as the other party is informed of the taping. Although some concerns have been voiced that tape-recordings may deter employees from making admissions during an examination, or from volunteering incriminating information about their co-workers, there are good reasons to record the proceeding. A tape-recording provides an objective, accurate account of the examination and also may be used to validate the length of the examination. This objective record may help disprove later claims of harassment during the examination. It also provides a record of any statements or admissions made during the test. It also may be used to confirm that the employee was provided with all oral notices required under the Act and regulations.

When should you inform an employee of his right to decline examination on medical grounds?

The Act and regulations require that the employee be informed of the right to decline examination on the written evidence of a physician, together with the other notices provided to the employee immediately prior to the examination. Nonetheless, it may be prudent to include this notice with the materials that are provided to the employee 48 hours prior to the examination in order to avoid a "last minute" attempt by the employee to invoke a medical excuse for not taking the examination. (For similar reasons, it may be prudent to provide early notice to an employee of the right to tape-record the examination. Indeed, employers may find it makes sense to include the entire notice attached as Appendix B with the materials provided to the employee 48 hours before the examination.)

Suppose an employee demands a polygraph test to "clear his name." Is it necessary to be concerned about the Act if an employee volunteers to take a polygraph test?

Yes. In an ongoing investigation of economic injury, an employee cannot be polygraphed—even if he or she asks to be tested—unless the employee had "access" to the property or activity that is the subject of the investigation, and the employer has sufficient evidence to demonstrate a "reasonable suspicion" of the employee's guilt. (Congress prohibited voluntary testing as a result of its concern that employees would be coerced into "voluntary" tests.)

Note: Whether an employee asks to be polygraphed or not, the employer must still comply with each and every procedural requirement of the law and regulations—including the notice provisions. Employers who have sufficient evidence to terminate an employee and who are prepared to discharge the employee without a polygraph test should exercise caution in responding to an employee's request for a polygraph test to prove his or her innocence; a procedural misstep in administering the test could jeopardize the discharge and subject the employer to a possible lawsuit, including a claim for reinstatement with back pay.

May an employer use the polygraph test to find out if an employee has been using illegal drugs at the workplace?

No. The polygraph may not be used to test for alcohol or drug use, even if alcohol or drug abuse is believed to have resulted in economic injury to the employer. The polygraph may be used, however, in an investigation of drug trafficking at the workplace, provided that the employer can demonstrate that such activities have resulted in economic harm to the employer. (Note: The newly-enacted Drug-free Workplace Act requires government contractors to establish and maintain procedures to ensure a drug-free workplace, and a contractor may be disbarred if found to have been lax in complying with this law.)

Does the Act prohibit an employer from using urinalysis tests to find out if an employee has been using illegal drugs?

No. The Act neither prohibits nor restricts the use of drug urinalysis tests for current employees or job applicants.

In the course of an investigation of sexual harassment, is it permissible to use a polygraph test to inquire into the sexual behavior of an employee?

No. During a polygraph examination, an employee may not be asked any questions concerning religious beliefs or affiliations, beliefs or opinions regarding racial matters, political beliefs or affiliations, or questions concerning "any matter relating to sexual behavior." This means that the polygraph must be carefully used, if at all, in the investigation of incidents with racial or religious overtones (for example, anonymous hate mail directed at minority workers). Moreover, the broad prohibition on questions concerning "any matter relating to sexual behavior" may make it impossible to use the polygraph in the investigation of sexual harassment complaints. (Note: The Act also prohibits questions concerning "beliefs, affiliations, opinions, or lawful activities regarding unions or labor organizations." The Act, therefore, does not prohibit the use of the polygraph to investigate acts of sabotage or violence, simply because they are related to a union organizing campaign.)

Does the Act allow an employer to use the polygraph in investigating the workplace theft of an employee's personal property?

In most cases, the answer to this question is "No." The polygraph may only be used in the course of an investigation of economic injury to the employer. Although this would include the theft of property entrusted to the employer's care (for example, the contents of a safe deposit box), it would not generally include acts of wrongdoing committed by one employee against another, unless it could be shown that these actions had resulted in economic injury to the employer. For example, if an employer indemnifies its workers against workplace thefts, the loss of an employee's property would be a loss to the employer.

May the employee's attorney or representative be excluded from the examination room during the actual test phase of the examination?

Yes. The Act gives the employee the right to consult with an attorney or employee representative "before each phase" of the examination, but the attorney or representative has no right to be present in the examination room during the examination. Moreover, it would appear that an employer could properly exclude an attorney or representative from each phase of the test—so long as an opportunity was provided to the employee to consult with his or her attorney before each phase of the test.

If new questions arise during an examination, may these questions be asked in a re-test of the employee, following the initial examination?

Yes, if the questions are first previewed with the employee. The law prohibits asking questions that have not been reviewed with the employee prior to the examination. However, polygraph examinations frequently consist of a series of tests. Where new questions arise, or where good practice dictates restructuring a question—nothing in the law would prohibit asking these questions to an employee on re-testing, provided that the questions are set down in writing and reviewed with the employee prior to the re-test. In such circumstances, especially if the changes concern "relevant" questions bearing on the subject of the investigation, the employee should be given the opportunity to consult with counsel prior to the re-test.

Note: If new questions arise after the conclusion of the examination, and the employee is to be called back for a second test on a later date, it would appear necessary for the employer to provide the employee—a second time—with all of the notices required by the law. This means, in particular, that the employee would have to be provided with forty-eight hours notice of the new examination.

May an employee be discharged or demoted on the basis of the results of a polygraph test (i.e., an analysis of a polygraph test chart)?

Yes, *but only with additional supporting evidence.* The evidence of "access" and "reasonable suspicion" accumulated to support administration of the polygraph test may be used to support a disciplinary action. In addition, the employer may use any statements or admissions made by the employee (or by other employees) before, during, or after a polygraph examination. Test results may not be used, however, even with supporting evidence, unless the employer has observed all of the procedural requirements of the law. (This answer assumes that the test is administered in connection with an "ongoing investigation" of economic injury to the employer.) Before any adverse employment action is taken, the employer must review the results of the polygraph test with the employee.

In the course of a legitimate workplace investigation, may an employee be discharged for refusing to take a polygraph test?

Yes, *but only with additional supporting evidence.* If the employer has sufficient evidence to demonstrate that an employee had "access" to the property or activity that is the subject of the investigation, and the employer can establish a "reasonable suspicion" of the employee's guilt, the employee may be terminated for refusing to take a polygraph test—even if the refusal is based on medical grounds. (This answer also assumes, of course, that the test is administered in connection with an "ongoing investigation" of economic injury to the employer, and that the employer complies with all of the procedural requirements of the Act and regulations.)

Can an employer be held liable for errors made by the polygraph examiner?

Yes. Moreover, if the polygraph examiner does not meet the qualifications for examiners established by the Act, the test results are subject to challenge and may be nullified. Employers should therefore exercise caution in hiring examiners, and should insist that the examiner certify his or her compliance with the Act and indemnify the employer for any liability arising out of errors or omissions by the examiner during the course of an examination.

GENERAL OBSERVATIONS The Employee Polygraph Protection Act preserves the opportunity for private sector employers to use the polygraph in the investigation of workplace wrongdoing. Nonetheless, the complexity of the Act and the regulations implementing the law argue strongly for consultation with legal counsel when use of the polygraph is contemplated in an investigation. Some small businesses, in particular, may find it prudent to abandon the polygraph, with its attendant risks of litigation, in favor of more conventional investigative tools. In all cases, employers should consider whether an investigation would better be pursued by law enforcement authorities (in some cases, notice to government agencies is mandatory), since the Act does not govern use of the polygraph by government agencies.

Selected Bibliography

Anderson, Ronald A. *Wharton's Criminal Law and Procedure.* Rochester, N.Y.: Rochester Lawyers Cooperative Publishing Co., 1957.

Astor, Saul D. *Loss Prevention: Controls and Concepts.* Los Angeles: Security World Publishing Co., Inc., 1978.

Barefoot, J. Kirk (ed.). *The Polygraph Story,* Revised Third Printing. Linthicum Heights, Md.: American Polygraph Association, October 1974.

Barefoot, J. Kirk. *Undercover Investigation,* Revised 2nd Edition. Stoneham, Mass.: Butterworths, 1983.

Buckwalter, Art. *Investigative Methods.* Stoneham, Mass.: Butterworths, 1984.

Ellis, Bill. "Proof of Loss in Fidelity Bond Claims," *Security World,* May 1978.

Kauffman, Robert M., Finerty, Gregory S., Eagan, James O., and Zimmerman, Robert M. *Retail Accounting and Financial Control,* Fifth Edition. New York: John Wiley, 1990.

Leininger, Sheryl (ed.). *Internal Theft: Investigation and Control.* Los Angeles: Security World Publishing Co., Inc., 1975.

Levy, Robert. "The Big Rip-Off in Purchasing," *Dun's Review,* March 1977.

Reid, John E., and Inbau, Fred E. *Truth and Deception: The Polygraph Technique,* Second Edition. Baltimore, Md.: Williams & Wilkins Co., 1976.

Sennewald, Charles. *The Process of Investigation.* Stoneham, Mass.: Butterworths, 1981.

Walsh, Timothy J., and Healy, Richard J. *Protection of Assets.* Santa Monica, Calif.: The Merritt Co., 1974.

Index